HARVARD LECTURES

ON

GREEK SUBJECTS

HARVARD LECTURES

ON

GREEK SUBJECTS

BY

S. H. BUTCHER

HON. D.LITT. OXFORD; HON. LITT.D. DUBLIN

HON. LL.D. GLASGOW AND EDINBURGH

LATE PROFESSOR OF GREEK IN THE UNIVERSITY OF EDINBURGH

FORMERLY FELLOW OF TRINITY COLLEGE, CAMBRIDGE

AND OF UNIVERSITY COLLEGE, OXFORD

London

MACMILLAN AND CO., LIMITED

NEW YORK: THE MACMILLAN COMPANY

1904

PREFACE

THESE Lectures—Public Lectures delivered at Harvard University in April 1904—owe their origin to a generous gift made to the University by Mr. Gardiner Martin Lane, of the Class of 1881; and will remain associated in my memory with the recollection of infinite kindness received during my visit to Cambridge and Boston.

The Lectures, here and there slightly expanded, are, in other respects, published almost in the form in which they were delivered. The hearers to whom they were originally addressed comprised not only classical scholars, but also

v

the general public ; and they are now offered
to a similarly mixed body of readers.

The book may be regarded as forming a
kind of companion volume to *Some Aspects of
the Greek Genius* (third edition, Macmillan
and Co. 1904). Under various lights I have
attempted to bring out something of the
originality of Greece. The contrast is at the
outset drawn between Greece and two older
civilisations :—that of Israel, dominated by a
great religious idea, and that of Phoenicia,
given over to the pursuit of material well-
being (I. and II.). In the subsequent lectures
two features of the Greek intellect come into
special prominence. First, a Love of Knowledge, which not only seeks out the facts of
nature and of man's life, but persistently asks
their meaning ; and this belief in the interpretative power of mind, working on and transmuting
all raw material of knowledge, is shown to

extend beyond the domain of philosophy or of science, and to give significance to Greek theories of history and Greek views on education (III.). Secondly, a Critical Faculty standing in singularly close relation to the Creative Faculty. Art and inspiration, logic and intuition, elsewhere so often disjoined, enter into perfect union in the constructive efforts of the Greek imagination. It is but one eminent example of that balance of contrasted qualities, that reconciliation of opposites, which meets us at every turn in the distinguished personalities of the Hellenic race, and which is too often thought of, in a merely negative way, as the avoidance of excess, rather than as the highest outcome of an intense and many-sided vitality (IV.). But the critical instinct, one of the primary endowments of the Greeks, operates also apart from the constructive power, and (chiefly from the time of Aristotle onwards) tries to penetrate the secret of the literary art. Here we have no longer the same sureness of insight ;—indeed the lack of it is frequently startling. Nevertheless there remains a sufficient body of interesting—and even illuminating— Criticism, to enable us to see, through Greek eyes, some of those literary principles of enduring value which Greece has bequeathed (V. and VI.).

S. H. BUTCHER.

October 1904.

CONTENTS

		PAGE
I.	GREECE AND ISRAEL	1
II.	GREECE AND PHOENICIA	44
III.	THE GREEK LOVE OF KNOWLEDGE	82
IV.	ART AND INSPIRATION IN GREEK POETRY	129
V.	GREEK LITERARY CRITICISM	169
VI.	GREEK LITERARY CRITICISM	219

ERRATUM

Page 101 note.   *For* κράτιστος *read* κρατίστη.

I

GREECE AND ISRAEL

Two nations, Greece and Israel, stand out from all others in the history of the world, and form a striking contrast as representing divergent impulses and tendencies of human nature, different ideals of perfection. In this, however, they are alike, that each felt itself to be a peculiar people, marked off from the surrounding races by distinctions more efface-able than those of blood—by the possession of intellectual or religious truths which deter-mined the bent and meaning of its history. That history, as it was gradually unfolded, became to each an unfailing source of inspira-tion. The records and famous deeds of the race were invested with ethical significance.

B

In interpreting them each people gained a
deeper consciousness of its own ideal vocation.
From the heritage of the past they drew fresh
stores of spiritual energy.   Exclusive indeed
they both were, intensely national ; between
Greeks and Barbarians, between Israel and the
Heathen there could be no intimacy, no union.
For many centuries the work of the Hellenes
and of Israel went forward at the same time,
but in separate spheres, each nation unconscious
of the other's existence.   Had they crossed
one another's path, they would have aroused
mutual hatred and suspicion ; the Jews would
have been barbarians to the Greeks, the Greeks
idolaters to the Jews.   Yet this very spirit of
exclusiveness was one of the conditions which
enabled each to nurture and bring to maturity
the life-giving germ which it bore within it.
In process of time each people burst the narrow
limits of its own nationality, and in dying to
itself, lived to mankind.   *Morientes vivimus*
is the epitome of each history.   The influence
by which both Jews and Greeks have acted on
all after ages is one which has survived the

outward forms of national existence ; it belongs
to the mysterious forces of the spirit.   Through
humiliation and loss of independence they each
entered on a career of world-wide empire, till
at length the principles of Hellenism became
those of civilisation itself, and the religion of
Judaea that of civilised humanity.

The Jews were from the outset conscious of
their separateness, of their peculiar mission.
From the family to the tribe, from the tribe to
the nation, they felt themselves to be destined
for some high purpose, though the idea was
deepened and expanded as their history
advanced.   With the Greeks it was otherwise.
In the Homeric age Greeks and Barbarians did
not yet stand sharply opposed ; and, though
during that period and long afterwards many
elements of foreign civilisations were slowly
absorbed, yet in the process of absorption they
were so transmuted that for the Hellenes the
net result was a heightened sense of difference
between themselves and the non-Hellenes.
The first impulse, however, towards national
unity came, as with the Jews, through religion.

The religious life of primitive Greece centred
at Dodona in Epirus, the seat of the oracle of
Zeus, of whose cult we catch a curious glimpse
in the famous invocation of Achilles (*Il.* xvi.
233). Dodona retained its immemorial sanctity
far into historical times ; but it never formed a
meeting-point for the scattered families of the
Hellenic race. At a very early date the Dodo-
naean cult gave place to the worship of Apollo,
who made his abode on the Eastern coast of
Greece, at Parnassus, with Delphi as his sanctuary. Zeus still remained the supreme god,
and Apollo, the youngest of the Olympians,
became his 'prophet,' his interpreter. The
tribal cults are henceforth merged in a higher
worship. A league of states representing the
common sentiment of the Hellenes is associated
with the Delphic shrine. Apollo here presides
at the Theoxenia—the festival celebrating the
friendship of the gods. In reconciling the
local deities he stands as the symbol of Hellenic
fraternity and union. The nobler energies of
the race now obtain a religious consecration.

The Delphic religion was in its highest

intention an effort after spiritual freedom and enlightenment. In this respect it offers a remarkable counterpart to Hebrew prophecy. It asserts the binding claim of the moral law alike over states and individuals. It deepens the conception both of guilt and purification. As the Hebrew prophets were charged with guarding the spiritual heritage of Israel, so the Pythian Apollo fostered the ideal of Hellenic character in religion, morality, and art. In speaking of Delphic prophecy we must dismiss the vulgar notion of merely predicting future events or revealing secrets. This lower art of soothsaying was, no doubt, in great demand in Greece at all periods of her history. Tablets discovered in Epirus in 1877 [1] give examples of the questions addressed by its rude votaries to the oracle of Dodona. A certain Agis asks about some lost property —mattresses and pillows—whether they may have been stolen by a stranger.[2] Another

---

[1] C. Carapanos, *Dodone et ses Ruines.*

[2] ἐπερωτεῖ Ἅγις Δία Νᾶον [καὶ Διώναν] ὑπὲρ τῶν στρωμάτων κ[αὶ τῶν προσ]κεφαλαίων, τὰ ἀπώλολ[εν] (? ἀπόλωλεν), ἢ τῶν ἔξωθέν τις ἂν ἔκ[λεψεν].

inquires whether the god advises sheep-farming as an investment.[1] Even at Delphi some of the responses recorded are trivial enough. But the influence of Delphi must not be judged by such isolated utterances. The ethical and civilising purpose it served is apparent to every attentive reader of Greek history and literature. Apollo's chief office is not to declare the future ; nor is he concerned with minute ceremonial observances. He bears a personal message to the people ; he is the expounder of the divine will ; it is part of his function to maintain an ethical ideal and to quicken the national consciousness. The pious inquirer at his shrine approaches him in the confidence of glad companionship, and holds converse with him as with a living personality. The mind of the supreme god is declared not in dark signs through the voices of nature or through perplexing dreams, but by human utterance and in rhythmical speech. Apollo, the προφήτης of Zeus, has human προφῆται of his own. But it is in accordance with the religion of Delphi to

---

[1] αἴ ἐστι αὐτοῖ προβατεύοντι ὤναιον καὶ ὠφέλιμον.

recognise not only a direct guidance from without, but also an inward revelation, telling of clear-felt duties and pointing to the god in the human breast. Apollo, speaking from the 'just-judging'[1] sanctuary, insists on inward motive, on purity of heart rather than on outward cleansing, on the spirit rather than on the letter of religion. He prefers the pious offering to the sumptuous sacrifice; he maintains the cause of the weak and the oppressed—of women, slaves, suppliants; he inculcates the duty of reverence for oaths. But he was also the familiar friend and counsellor of the nation. He took into his keeping the civic life of Greece. Under Delphic supervision the colonial system was organised, and missionaries of Greek culture were settled in every land. The express sanction of the Delphic oracle was sought for the founding of colonies, such as Byzantium, Syracuse, Cyrene. Apollo, moreover, was invested with all the gracious attributes of knowledge and artistic skill. He was the god of science, of art, of poetry; he presided

[1] Pind. *Pyth.* xi. 9.

at the games and festivals. Under his influence were developed the contrasted ideals that mark the type of Hellene and of Barbarian—the Hellene with his self-knowledge and self-control ; his love of ordered freedom ; his belief in reason and in the supremacy of the spirit over the senses : the Barbarian glorying in brute force, with blind impulses carrying him now towards anarchy, now towards slavery, unconscious of moral limitations, overstepping the bounds of law and reverence.

I am speaking of the Delphic worship on its ideal side, apart from the inherent unrealities and corruptions in which it was embedded. Yet, even from this point of view, there are striking differences as well as resemblances between Delphic and Jewish prophecy. The Delphic priestess, seized and subdued by an apparently divine possession, lifted out of herself in transport, presents a contrast to the Hebrew prophet whose reason and senses remain undisturbed under stress of inspiration. The familiar attitude, also, of the Greek towards his god is as unlike as can be to the distant and awful

communion which the Hebrew prophet holds
with the Almighty.   Nor again does the history
of the Hebrew prophets afford any parallel to
the defection of Delphi from the national cause.
Even before the Persian wars Delphi had more
than once yielded to the temptations which
beset an ambitious priesthood.   Now, at the
supreme crisis of the nation's history, she could
not rise above timid and temporising counsels.
She was, it must be owned, forced to make
a difficult choice.   Her connexions over the
barbarian world were widely extended. The gifts
of the East flowed in on her.   Phrygia and
Lydia were among her clients.   Her material
interests forbade her to pronounce the clear
word which would have put her at the head
of Greek resistance to the barbarians.   And so,
the place, which from the eighth century onward
she had held as the recognised conscience of
Greece, she now forfeited and never wholly
regained.   In politics, the championship of
the Panhellenic cause was assumed by Athens ;
and outside the political sphere, it devolved
more and more on poets and philosophers to

perpetuate the Delphic tradition by an effort to spiritualise the popular creed and reconcile it with a purer morality. The case of the Hebrew prophets is one of marked contrast. They never ceased to be the guardians of an ideal national sentiment. Not that they merely reflected prevalent opinion. If in a sense they were the spokesmen of the nation, they became so only by combating the will and denouncing the vices of their fellow-countrymen. Between prophets and people there was an unending conflict. We speak of the monotheism of the Jews; yet they were ever prone to idolatry, being recalled from it only by warning and disasters. We speak of their spiritual faculty; yet who more carnal than they?—lovers of pleasure, lovers of ease, lovers of money. Again and again they were saved from themselves only by their inspired teachers, by the austere voice of prophecy.

There were moments when religion stood opposed—as one might think—to a larger patriotism; and the prophets had to bear the hard reproach of appearing anti-national.

Jeremiah was cast into prison as a traitor.
Two conflicting tendencies, as Renan has shown,
were at work within Judaism : one, to mix with
other nations and learn the ways of the world ;
the other, to shun all contact with alien civilisations—art, commerce, foreign alliances being
regarded as so many dangers which might
detach the people from their true allegiance.
The first policy—that of expansion—was the
policy of the kings ; the second, the policy of
the prophets. The attitude of the prophets
towards outside movements and influences was
one of extreme circumspection or distrust. But
the narrower—we might be inclined to say the
more illiberal view—was, after all, the truly
national one. Once we grant that the peculiar
mission of Israel was to guard the principle of
monotheism, and that any premature attempt at
expansion would have meant absorption into
heathendom, it follows that the pursuit of
secular aims and of a many-sided development
would have been for the nation the abandon-
ment of her high calling.

Delphi in her earlier and better days was

more happily placed in relation to outside currents of thought. Vividly conscious though she was of the antithesis between Greeks and Barbarians, no timid fears that Hellenism might be lost in barbarism checked her forward energies. Greece must not be kept out of the general movement of the world. Rather it was dimly felt that the world was one day to be hellenised. The idea that is openly expressed in the fourth century B.C. of a larger Hellenism resting not on racial but on spiritual affinities seems to have floated vaguely before the mind at an earlier date. Delphi was long able to pursue a policy of progress and expansion without endangering either patriotism or religion.

Here we strike on the fundamental difference between Hebrews and Greeks—the Hebrews preoccupied, dominated by a single idea, and that a religious one ; the Greeks moved by the impulse for manifold culture. Two distinct individualities stand out in clear relief. To the Hebrews it was committed to proclaim to mankind the one and supreme God, to keep alive his pure worship, to assert the inexorable moral

law in a corrupt and heathen world. For the
Greeks the paramount end was the perfection
of the whole nature, the unfolding of every
power and capacity, the complete equipment of
the man and of the citizen for secular existence.
The Hebrews had no achievement to show in
the purely secular sphere of thought and conduct. They had no art,—if we except music—
no science, no philosophy, no organised political
life, no civic activity, no public spirit. In
regard to plastic representation, they were pure
iconoclasts ; for idolatry was a danger near and
menacing. The search for causes—the inspiring principle of the scientific spirit—was for
them either an idle occupation of which man
soon wearies, as in *Ecclesiastes*, or an encroach-
ment on the rights of God. The discovery of
a reign of law in nature, which to the Ionians
of the sixth century B.C. seemed the highest
function of the human intellect, was alien to
the Hebrew mode of thought.

Poetry indeed they had, unique in its kind :
the lyrical utterances of the Psalms, outpourings
of religious emotion unsurpassed, or rather un-

approached, in depth and range of feeling ; that
sublime drama, again, or dramatic lyric, the
Book of Job ; the apocalyptic visions of the
prophets, revealed in words such as those which
Isaiah the son of Amos ' saw.' Yet if we except the idyll of the *Book of Ruth* and the *Song
of Solomon*—a beautiful and human love-song,
which stands in such curious isolation from
the other contents of the volume with which it
is bound up—Hebrew poetry is of a different
order from that of our Western civilisation ; it is
poetry lifted into another sphere and made one
with religion. The epic, and the drama in its
strict sense, are wanting. We have not the
laughter as well as the tears of humanity ; no
airy structures of the fancy ; none of the playful
ironies of existence ; no half lights or subtle
undertones ; none of the rich variety of poetry in
its graceful and intermediate forms. The world
which Hebrew poetry reproduces is not a second
world recreated out of the elements of the actual,
though separate from reality — a region into
which we are transported by the power of imaginative sympathy. It is the actual world itself.

The two living realities, God and the Soul, are face to face, engaged in everlasting colloquy. We overhear voices of pleading and warning, of pathos and hope, of repentance and forgiveness. And as with the individual so with the nation. All the spiritual experiences of the race, as summed up in an unforgotten past, are expressed in language instinct with poetic emotion.

In Hebrew poetry there is a pervading sublimity which has no precise parallel in any other literature. To the Greek poet, 'Wonders are many and nothing is more wonderful than man': yet marvellous as are the achievements of man's art and skill, his daring courage, his civic inventiveness, all fall short of the moral sublimity he attains through suffering, by the endurance of god-sent calamity, and by an unconquerable will. In Hebrew poetry, lyrical and descriptive, the note of sublimity is of a different kind. It belongs to the domain of heaven. Man is in himself 'a thing of nought,' 'even as a dream when one awaketh'; feeble and perishable; vicissitude and decay are stamped on his terrestrial life. 'The earth shall reel to and fro

like a drunkard, and shall be removed like a
cottage.'   At the sight of the majestic order of
the universe, still more in the contemplation of
God's everlasting righteousness, his unsearchable
greatness, there arises a sense of awe-struck
exultation.   'The Lord is King, the earth may
be glad thereof : yea the multitude of the isles
may be glad thereof.   Clouds and darkness are
round about him : righteousness and judgment
are the habitation of his seat.'   'The Lord sitteth
above the water-flood : the Lord remaineth a
King for ever.'   Essentially sublime, too, are
the descriptions which suggest the omnipotence
of the divine word.   'And God said, Let
there be light : and there was light.'   'For
he spake and it was done : he commanded
and it stood fast.'   'Where wast thou when
I laid the foundations of the earth ? declare,
if thou hast understanding. . . . Or who laid
the corner stone thereof, when the morning
stars sang together, and all the sons of God
shouted for joy ?   Or who shut up the sea
with doors . . . and said, Hitherto shalt thou
come, but no further ; and here shall thy proud

waves be stayed?' He who 'commandeth the sun and it riseth not, and sealeth up the stars.'

Greek poetry in its more serious forms is almost as deeply penetrated with theology as is Hebrew poetry with religion. The Hebrew poets seldom dare to dwell upon those problems touching the moral government of the world which exercised a grave fascination over the imaginative mind of Greece. Yet at times some troubled reflections escape their lips, as in the *Psalms*, or in shorter outbursts of lyrical emotion. In one book, however, of the Bible the cry of humanity utters itself in tones of reasoned rebellion and with unique audacity. The *Book of Job* and the *Prometheus* of Aeschylus may be placed side by side, as the two protests of the ancient world against divine oppression—the one the protest of monotheism, the other of polytheism. Let us glance for a moment at these two poems. They form a luminous comment on the contrasted spirit of the two nations.

The character of Zeus in the *Prometheus* exhibits every line and colour of tyranny as it

C

was understood by the Greeks. Zeus is the 'new lord,'[1] enforcing his will by relentless ministers, 'ruling by his own laws,'[2] 'keeping justice in his own hands,'[3] 'a harsh monarch and irresponsible,'[4] distrustful of his friends,[5] malevolent towards his subjects, ungrateful to those who had done him service. Even his friends do not question the judgment of his foes. His character is thrown into yet darker shade by the appearance in the play of Io, in whose history is recorded one of the distinctive marks of the tyrant—a selfish and heartless love. The two sufferers, Io and Prometheus, meet by chance on the rocks of Scythia, the one the victim of the love of Zeus, the other of his hate ; the one the very emblem of restless movement, the other of a chained captivity. In various details, moreover, the old legend is so modified as to place in strong relief the beneficent effects of Prometheus' revolt. A single point may be

---

[1] *Prom.* 96 νέος ταγός, cp. 149, 310, 389, 955.

[2] *Ib.* 403 ἰδίοις νόμοις κρατύνων.

[3] *Ib.* 187 παρ' ἑαυτῷ τὸ δίκαιον ἔχων.

[4] *Ib.* 324 τραχὺς μόναρχος οὐδ' ὑπεύθυνος κρατεῖ, cp. 35.

[5] *Ib.* 224-225.

mentioned. In Hesiod the theft of fire leads
indirectly to all the evils that flesh inherits.
Till then, under the rule of Cronus men were
as gods enjoying all happiness—ὥστε θεοὶ
δ' ἔζωον. In the train of civilisation came all
manner of woes and sicknesses. It was as it
were the Fall of man. The age of ignorance
was the age of gold. In Aeschylus, by the act
of Prometheus, the human race so far from
forfeiting a state of primitive well-being, rises
for the first time out of a feeble, timorous existence ; it subdues to its own use the forces of
nature ; 'blind hopes' are planted in man's
heart—the pledge of future progress. Nor did
Prometheus, as some would have it, by an act
of impatient philanthropy forestall the wise
purposes of Zeus. The design of Zeus was to
sweep away the race. Prometheus, therefore,
rescued man not merely from a life of brute
stagnation, but from death itself.

Many critics have maintained that in ranging
ourselves on the side of Prometheus against
Zeus we are interpreting the drama in a modern
sense and in a manner alien to the thought of

Aeschylus.   But the character of the benefactor
is drawn in outlines no less firm than that of
the oppressor of mankind ; and the words in
which Prometheus sums up his own history
accord with all the facts of the dramatic
presentation : ' In chains ye see me, an ill-fated
god, the foe of Zeus, *because I loved mortals
overmuch* ' (διὰ τὴν λίαν φιλότητα βροτῶν).[1]
Prometheus embodies the Greek type of moral
heroism as truly as Zeus does that of tyranny.
The hero of Greek poetry, the hero as Athens
loved to portray him, is not only eminent for
courage or indomitable in his will-power ; he is
also generous in sympathy ; pitiful to the weak ;
moved by a chivalrous, a romantic impulse to
redress the wrongs of the world.   Prometheus
unites the two sides of the heroic character.
He is tender as well as magnanimous.   ' Out
of the strong came forth sweetness.'   Towards
the Ocean Nymphs he shows a delicate and
gentle courtesy.   The tormented and confiding
Io pours her woe into his ear ; and the sublime
sorrow of the god finds room within it for the

[1] *Prom.* 119-122.

plaintive outpourings of the mortal. And, as
'love overmuch' has been his fault, so all
creation, animate and inanimate, mourns in
sympathy with him in the splendid chorus, lines
397-435.

If this, then, is the true reading of the play,
it presents the struggle between two wills, each
equally unyielding, the one strong in the consciousness of physical power, the other in moral
greatness and wisdom. That Aeschylus should
have placed Zeus in such a light before an
Athenian audience, has seemed to many readers
an impiety so daring as to be impossible. But
let us not lose sight of the far-off period at
which the action is imaginatively laid. The
Aeschylean heroes are often men in whose veins
the blood of gods still runs—

κοὔπω σφιν ἐξίτηλον αἷμα δαιμόνων.[1]

In this play they are not godlike men but
actual gods. We are carried back to an age
anterior even to the action of the *Iliad*. One
dynasty of gods has overthrown another, but
not without the rough and lawless deeds which

[1] Aesch. Fr. 146.

accompany such a change.　The sovereignty of
Zeus is as yet insecure.　The 'new lord' of
Olympus has had a beginning ; he will also have
an end unless he mends his ways of governing.
The shadow of dispossession hangs over him.
He is subject to a mysterious power stronger
than himself ; between his will and the supreme
Fate there is still a discord.　His omnipotence
is limited by this control.　So far is he from
being omniscient that he is ignorant of the
secret on which the permanence of his throne
depends.　His reign is stained by caprice and
crime.　This is surely not the same Zeus that
is elsewhere called in Aeschylus, 'king of
kings,' 'most blessed of the blest,' 'all-seeing,'
'who rewards all men according to their works,'
'who guides men in the path of wisdom.'
Rather, he represents a passing epoch ; he is the
ruler of the visible order of things in an era
when might and right are not yet reconciled.
The play itself looks forward to a future which
shall adjust the disorders of the present.　We
cannot here discuss the difficult question of the
sequel ; but once we admit that within the

mythological framework of the Greek religion
the supreme god might be exhibited as subject
to a law of development, and as growing from
lawlessness into righteousness ; that even for
Zeus Time could be the great Teacher, in the
full significance of Prometheus' words—

ἀλλ' ἐκδιδάσκει πάνθ' ὁ γηράσκων χρόνος [1]—

then, many of the elements for the future
reconciliation are ready to hand.   As Aeschylus
elsewhere sets the Eumenides against Apollo, the
old against the new, so in the *Prometheus* does
he set Zeus against the Titan, the new against
the old.   In each case the strife must be resolved
in a final harmony.   In the *Prometheus*, the
sovereignty of the supreme god becomes
assured only when Wisdom and Power shall
have entered into indissoluble union.   Wisdom
without Power is ineffectual : Power without
Wisdom, though it may last for a time, cannot
be enthroned as immortal.[2]   This is probably

[1] *Prom.* 981.

[2] This view of the *Prometheus*, which I have placed before
my pupils for more than twenty years, is, I find, supported by
the authority of so eminent a scholar as Dissen, in a letter to
Welcker printed in Welcker's *Trilogie* 1824 ; see an interesting

the explanation of what at first sight seems
the most daring audacity ever enacted on the
Greek stage. The mind of Aeschylus loved
to move among the dim forms of the elder
world. Before his vision gods in their succession
came and went. Viewed in the immense
perspective of the past the sway of these gods
was almost as ephemeral as that of mortals.
With them too the higher displaced the lower.
Their story, like that of humanity, was one of
moral growth. There was a law of evolution,
a process of becoming, from which even deity
was not exempt. To Aeschylus the dramatist
no theme could well have been more congenial
than that of the *Prometheus*, giving scope, as it
did, for a conflict of will-power on a scale of
such colossal grandeur. But Aeschylus the
profoundly religious theologian would surely
have shrunk from a dramatic situation so
perilous to piety, were it not that the fluid
and ever-shifting forms of Greek mythology

article in the *Classical Review*, March 1904, by Janet Case. Also
it has been ably and independently put forward by Professor
Lewis Campbell in his introduction to the *Prometheus Bound*
(1890).

lent themselves to the utmost freedom of poetic handling.

In passing to the *Book of Job*, we observe some points of detailed resemblance in the setting of the two poems.   Just as Prometheus at the outset maintains silence——one of those eloquent Aeschylean silences——so too Job held his peace ' seven days and seven nights ' ; and then, like Prometheus, reviews his life, proudly proclaiming his own innocence.   His friends seek to convince him that he has done wrong. They cannot extort from him the admission. As compared with other men he knows himself to be guiltless.   And as the chief actors use similar language about themselves, the language they use about the deity is also in some degree similar.   In Prometheus it is an expression of proud defiance towards one whom he regards as a tyrant and an upstart, and whose future overthrow he calmly contemplates.   In Job, the voice of accusation seems to touch more nearly on blasphemy, as addressed to a God who was not only supreme, but in the highest sense righteous.   It is, however, this very

perfection of power and goodness which adds a
sting to the apparent injustice. The feeling is
one of conflict and strange perplexity. Almost
in the same breath with passionate remonstrance
and complaint there come accents of trust and
utter self-surrender. It is the sort of irony
which belongs to love. In form an accusation
it is in reality an expression of belief in the
very attributes that are denied, an appeal to
the deity to remove the inconsistencies which
seem to darken his character, to explain
the flaws in his own work, to reconcile his
goodness and his power. Hence the sudden
transitions and alternations of mood. Now God
is a hard adversary ; for man to plead against
him is despair : yet plead he will, though it
should be at the cost of his life (ch. ix. 20-
21). ' Thou knowest that I am not wicked '
(ch. x. 7); 'is it good unto thee that thou
shouldest oppress ? ' (ch. x. 3). In his anguish
God and his enemies seem ranged on one side
(ch. xvi. 7-16). But again by a sudden revulsion
of feeling he turns to God, whom he invokes
to be judge in his own cause ; he makes him

his arbiter even while he is his adversary: 'Even now, behold, my witness is in heaven, and he that voucheth for me is on high' (ch. xvi. 19 Rev. Vers.). He complains that God hides from him, that he is not in the East nor in the West. 'Oh that I knew where I might find him! that I might come even to his seat! I would order my cause before him.' 'When he hath tried me, I shall come forth as gold' (ch. xxiii. 1-10). 'Now I have ordered my cause; I know that I shall be justified' (ch. xiii. 18). The sense of ill treatment and despair is heightened in Job's case by a special circumstance. Whereas Prometheus is conscious that he is an immortal and that his victory in the future is assured, Job has no clear belief in immortality. At the most, it stands out dimly as a hope. The old patriarchal theory of life was in need of no hereafter. The good man was always rewarded, the bad man punished. But the theory was giving way; it was discredited by experience; and with the blank so created the whole scheme of things fell into confusion. For commonplace minds, such as Job's friends,

the old formulas still sufficed. But to those
who looked steadily on life the discord between
merit and reward was apparent. How account
for the divine misrule? There are moments
when Job hints, as it would seem, at a life hereafter as the key to these moral problems; but
such rare glimpses are soon lost in deeper
darkness.

The endings of the two poems are signifi-
cantly different. The decisive contrast lies in
the characters of the two deities whose justice
has been impugned. The God who is the
antagonist of Prometheus has power, but he has
not goodness: the God who is the antagonist
of Job is perfect in goodness as in power. And
so Prometheus, strong in conscious right and in
foreknowledge of the future, remains unshaken
by persuasions and threats. At the close of the
drama, from out of elemental ruin——earthquake
and lightning and tempest——he utters his last
defiant words: 'Thou seest what unjust things
I suffer.' Job, who in all his troubled question-
ings has never lost his central trust in the God
whom he has upbraided, ends by a retractation:

' I know that thou canst do all things, and that
no purpose of thine can be restrained . . . I
have uttered that which I understood not,
things too wonderful for me, which I knew
not' (ch. xlii. 2, 3 Rev. Vers.). The infinite
mysteries of creation, as they are flashed before
him in a series of sublime descriptions (ch. xxviii.-
xli.), have subdued the heart as well as the intellect. Love, dormant throughout, is now fully
awakened. Yet even for Job the bewildering
problem remained unsolved. Jehovah's answer
had merely shown him Nature's immensity and
the nothingness of Man.

While philosophy had for the Jews no meaning, history had a deeper significance than it
bore to any other people. It was the chief
factor in their national unity, the source from
which they drew ethical and spiritual enlightenment. Thither they turned as to living oracles
inscribed with the finger of the Almighty. To
history they appealed as the supreme tribunal
of God's justice. Nor was the history of their
past merely a possession of their own ; it was
a treasure they held in trust for the human race.

The story of the Jews was part and parcel of the ' book of the generations of man.' Before the eyes of the prophets history as a whole emerged as an orderly plan, conceived in the counsels of the eternal, slowly unfolding itself in the rise and fall of empires, in startling catastrophes, in sharp and swift punishments which smite the innocent with the guilty ; but not less in the normal processes of a nation's life, its growth, its decay, its obedience, its rebellion, in the seed-time and harvest of the moral world. The great monarchies, Egypt, Assyria, Babylonia, Persia, pass across the scene. Their fortunes cross and interlock with those of the chosen race. Israel is the pivot on which their destiny turns. In their pride they boast of victories not their own. The Assyrian says ' By the strength of my hand I have done it, and by my wisdom ' ; but they are each an instrument, though they know it not, in the hands of the Almighty, by which he chastises his forgetful people or re-admits them to his favour. History, in a word, is the drama in which God himself is the protagonist, vindicating his justice and moral government on the stage of the visible world.

Never has any people been so conscious of its own spiritual calling as the Jews ; none has had so profound an intuition of the future. They pondered their long preparation and equipment for their office, its unique design, their repeated lapses, their baffled hopes, the promises postponed. The outward trappings of national existence fell away. All that constitutes history in the eyes of secular nations —war and politics, the deeds of kings, heroic struggles for independence—these things occupied an ever lessening space in their annals ; their only life was the indestructible life of the spirit. They were content to suffer and to wait. They had all the tenacity of hope. Disencumbered of material greatness, they enlisted themselves on the side of purely spiritual forces. It was the prerogative of their race to be 'an ensign to the nations,' to bear the banner of the true God.

The only Greek historian whose philosophy of history recalls in some chief features that of

the Jewish Scriptures is Herodotus.   To him
the course of the world, its incidents great and
small, are under divine governance.   The same
' forethought '[1] or providence which is at work in
maintaining a just balance of forces within the
animal kingdom, likewise presides over the
destiny of empires.   This supreme power reveals
its will through various modes of utterance—
through oracular voices, through signs, through
disturbances in the physical order of nature.
It humiliates human pride, it lures on insolence
to its ruin, it pursues the guilty through generations.   And as in Jewish history the fortunes
of Israel intermingle with the secular currents
of universal history, so in Herodotus Greek
history is read in its larger and world-wide
relations.   The great military monarchies pass
before our eyes in a series of apparent digressions ;
but the main theme is never forgotten ; the
tragic action moves onward through retarding
incidents, till at last the divine retribution
hastens towards its goal, and all the pride of
the East, gathered into one under Persia, flings

[1] προνοίη, Herod. iii. 108.

itself in preordained ruin on the free land of Hellas.

The problems of politics never exercised the mind of Israel. No questions arose about royalty, aristocracy, or democracy, as entitled to put forward their several claims ; there was no thought of tempering the evils of unmixed or extreme constitutions, or of harmonising conflicting ideals, such as at an early period seized upon the reflective spirit of Greece. The Jewish wars of liberation were waged not for political, but for religious freedom. It has been remarked by Renan that the Jews accepted with easy acquiescence any political régime which, like that of Persia, was fairly tolerant of their religious worship. On the other hand, the mind of Israel, ill-fitted indeed to found a secular state, or to adjust the various functions of government, went out in aspiration towards the citizenship of a larger country. The oneness of God carried with it, as an implicit consequence, the oneness of humanity. Even the law, though in the first instance a covenant with a single people, and in spite of its minor

D

enactments and disciplinary rules, itself became
a unifying power.   Its moral precepts, flowing
from one God as the sole source of law, had
a universal and binding force.   And if the
demands of the law knew no restriction of race,
so its privileges were open to all.   No ancient
constitution accorded to strangers such a
position as they enjoyed under the Mosaic code.
At Athens resident aliens received a more
humane and favoured treatment than in any
other state in Greece.   Still, even there, they
had no legal or civic status ; access to the courts
was secured to them only through the service
of a patron ; and though this measure of
recognition may be put down in part to Attic
φιλανθρωπία or kindliness, the direct motive
undoubtedly was a commercial one.   With the
Jews the rights of the alien are placed on a
clear religious basis—the unity of God involving
the brotherhood of man.   ' Ye shall have one
manner of law, as well for the stranger, as for
one of your own country : for I am the Lord
your God' (Lev. xxiv. 22).   The declaration
that 'God loveth the stranger' (Deut. x. 18)

involved far-reaching consequences which cannot be extracted from the kindly religious sentiment expressed in the Homeric words, 'the stranger and the beggar are from Zeus.' The lessons, moreover, of suffering and the memory of the house of bondage are brought in to reinforce the ethical duty. 'Thou shalt love him as thyself; for ye were strangers in the land of Egypt' (*Lev.* xix. 34). At the heart of Judaism beneath its hard and often repelling exclusiveness the idea of universal humanity was being matured. With the preaching of the prophets in the eighth century Judaism became essentially a social religion, a religion of humanity. In the last days of the kingdom of Judah the feeling of compassion for the weak, of sympathy for the poor and the oppressed, takes a deeper and tenderer tone. The sense of the inequalities of life strike in upon the mind with a new and piercing force. 'To undo the heavy burdens and let the oppressed go free'; 'to open the eyes of the blind'; 'to satisfy the afflicted soul'; to deliver suffering humanity from the darkness of the prison-house—this

became the absorbing passion of the Hebrew.
Such a moral enthusiasm could recognise no
restrictions of age or country.   In a regenerate
society, and under the law of the spiritual kingdom foreshadowed by the prophets, all barriers
must be broken down.   The families of the
earth, already united by a common origin, are
henceforth to be united by a common hope.
' For my house shall be called an house of
prayer for all people.'

Greek thinkers no less than Hebrew prophets
figure to their imagination an ideal society.   In
Plato's *Republic* justice finds an earthly home.
The outward fabric and framework of the city
are essentially of the Hellenic type.   In its
laws and bye-laws, as distinct from the moral
principles on which it is based, it is subject to
the usual Hellenic limitations—with, indeed, one
notable exception, that war between Hellenes
is forbidden, and that one Hellenic state may
not enslave another.   But the distinction
between Greeks and barbarians is retained ; and
within the city sharp lines of demarcation are
drawn.   There are full citizens, for the sake of

whose complete training in virtue and intellect the state exists; the governing power resides in their hands; but beyond these there is a great disinherited class, of traders and artisans who are not true members but only parts of the community, and of slaves who are mere instruments for carrying out their masters' will.

So far Plato does not rise above his own age and country. But his real concern is not with the external organisation of the state. The secret he desires to discover is the true method of training intellect and character:—how human nature may be moulded into the form of perfect goodness; how the highest natural endowments, the love of beauty, which reveals the world of art and literature, and the love of truth, which makes man one with himself and one with his fellow-men, may be fostered and combined. Plato is under no illusions as to any facile mode of reforming society. The high hopes of early youth had been shattered. The lesson of Greek history was to him full of despair. Selfishness and corruption, the inordinate assertion of the individual without regard to the welfare of the whole—this was what confronted him in civic life. The thinking man who shrinks from engaging in the turmoil of faction may well be tempted to 'hold his peace and do his own business,' 'content if only he can live his own life and be pure from evil or unrighteousness, and depart in peace and good will with bright hopes.'[1]

No merely external changes could restore a society so deeply corrupt. Until wisdom and beneficence, knowledge and power—the power of government combined with true philosophic insight—were united in the same persons, mankind could have no release from evil. We are reminded of the union foreshadowed in the *Prometheus* of power and goodness in the government of Olympus. Plato is bent on arriving at an intellectual apprehension of the moral forces which underlie all political and social improvement. On the one hand he traces the ascent of the soul, of the nobler philosophic nature, from the darkness to the light, and studies the law of its upward progress ; on the

[1] *Rep.* vi. 496 D–E.

other hand he gives a penetrating psychological
analysis of the successive stages of moral decline
both in states and individuals.   The fervour
with which he describes the power of philosophy
to raise and transform life, to bring thought
and action into harmony, has the glow of
religious emotion.   His words fall little short
of Hebrew prophecy in their intensity.   But
let us not mistake his drift and purpose.   He
has not the directly operative aim of the social
reformer.   He is not seeking to ameliorate the
outward conditions of existence, or to raise the
lot of the poor and struggling.   He is well
aware that the earthly state, in which he seeks
to embody his highest conception of justice or
human goodness, is an ideal, and that the
pattern of his city is 'laid up in the heavens.'
The regeneration of society stands out before
him as a far-off hope.   He strains his eyes after
the heavenly vision, but it is the vision of a
philosopher not a prophet, of one who is 'the
spectator of all time and all being'; for whom
the laws of truth and conduct are the great
primary reality, towards which the mind must

strive in far-reaching aspiration, though no era
of righteousness is as yet dawning on the world.
Yet he insists that the ideal is none the worse
for being merely an ideal. His belief never
wavers in the sovereignty of reason, in the
affinity of the human soul to the divine, and in
the vision of the Good as the illuminating power
of human life. It is the business of the
philosopher to open the eyes and to direct the
groping steps of the multitude. ' Could they
see the philosopher as he is, they would
certainly accept him for their guide.'

The vision of the prophets differed from the
vision even of the greatest of the philosophers
in the ever increasing clearness with which its
reality was apprehended. The spirit of hope, so
distinctive of the Jewish people, the invincible
optimism which survived every disappointment,
sustained them to the last. They laid hold of
the future as their own possession, with a confidence unapproached by any other nation, unless
we may find a distant parallel in the exhilaration
of tone with which the Roman poets forecast
the imperial greatness of Rome. To the Greeks

the future is dim and inscrutable; poets and prose writers repeat with many variations the sad refrain, 'uncertain is the future'[1]—ἄδηλον τὸ μέλλον. 'Forecasts of the future,' says Pindar, 'have been doomed to blindness.'[1] The future is the secret belonging to the gods, and it were presumptuous for man to seek to penetrate it. His duty is to seize the present with its limitless possibilities, and to use it with that rational energy and forethought which are born of an enlightened experience. It is a temper of mind wholly unlike that of the Jew, the loss of whose earthly country seemed to point him forward with a more victorious certitude to 'the city which hath foundations,' to the Heavenly Jerusalem.

'He hath set Eternity in their heart':[2] so might we sum up the spirit of Israel. But the Jewish ideal simplified life by leaving half of it untouched. It remained for Greece to make the earth a home, ordered and well equipped for

---

[1] Pind. *Ol.* viii. ad init.   τῶν δὲ μελλόντων τετύφλωνται φραδαί. (Trans. Jebb.)

[2] *Ecclesiastes* iii. 11 (margin).

the race, if not indeed for the individual.   Greece
supplied the lacking elements—art, science,
secular poetry, philosophy, political life, social
intercourse.   The matchless force of the Greek
mind and its success in so many fields of human
activity is, as we shall see, due above all to this,
that it was able harmoniously to combine diverse
and even opposite qualities.   Hebraism and
Hellenism stand out distinct, the one in all the
intensity of its religious life, the other in the
wealth and diversity of its secular gifts and
graces.

> Thus the sharp contrasts of the sculptor's plan
>   Showed the two primal paths our race has trod ;—
> Hellas the nurse of man complete as man,
>   Judaea pregnant with the living God.

I do not ask you to estimate the value of these
two factors, one against the other, to compare
things so incommensurable.   Each people is at
once the historical counterpart and the supplement of the other.   Each element, by contribut-
ing its own portion to our common Christianity,
has added to the inalienable treasure of the
world.   For the present, however, our immediate

concern is with Greece. Within these walls
the Hellenes are, I imagine, a small and peculiar
people; though not, I hope, a dwindling
minority. Outside are the larger ranks of the
non-Hellenes—I hardly like to call them by
their Greek title, the Barbarians. But the
Hellenes, like the Hebrews, have always prevailed by the few, not by the many. Nor
was it till ancient Hellas ceased to be an
independent nation that it became one of the
moving forces of the world's history. With
the Greeks, as with the Hebrews, the days of
their abasement have once and again preceded
their greatest triumphs; the moment of apparent
overthrow has been the starting-point for fresh
spiritual or intellectual conquest. That is a
cheering omen when we are asked to believe
that the study of Greek is now an anachronism,
and out of keeping with our progressive civilisation.

II

GREECE AND PHOENICIA

IN this lecture I propose to place side by side two contrasted civilisations—that of Phoenicia and that of Greece. The history of Phoenicia centres mainly round the names of the great commercial cities of Sidon, Tyre, and at a later period Carthage. I need not remind you that the Phoenicians were the pioneers of civilisation in the Mediterranean, and did the carrying trade of the ancient world. They perfected the industrial discoveries of earlier nations, exhibiting singular resource and ingenuity in developing such arts as pottery, glass-making, gold-working, and the like. But they also started new branches of industry of their own, and, in particular, by the discovery of the purple dye, established an immense trade in textile fabrics.

Fearless and patient navigators and explorers, they felt their way along the stepping-stones of the Greek archipelago till they pushed to the furthest limits of the known world. Their settlements extended over the whole Aegean, along the African coast and the western Mediterranean, and thence to the Atlantic; they traded from the coasts of Britain to those of North-West India. Phoenicia was the 'mart of nations'; 'whose merchants' were 'princes, whose traffickers' were 'the honourable of the earth.'[1] In the earliest glimpse we get of them we see their mariners touching at every shore, exchanging their manufactured articles for the natural products of the country, and at each point shipping some new cargo for their homeward voyage. Overtaken by winter on a distant coast, they would quietly wait there till the return of spring enabled them to sail on calmer seas. They opened up trade routes for overland as well as maritime commerce. The Phoenician merchant would penetrate into African deserts or exile himself

[1] *Isaiah* xxiii. 2, 8.

for years in the bazaars of Nineveh or Babylon
to extend his markets. Starting from the
coast of Palestine, a mere handful of men, this
people created a world-wide commerce, maintained themselves in scattered groups among
unfriendly populations, holding the very out-
posts of civilisation, and laid the foundation of
a great colonial dominion. About 600 B.C.
Tyrian sailors, despatched on a mission by
Pharaoh Necho of Egypt, are said to have
doubled the Cape of Good Hope and circum-
navigated Africa.

'Those English of antiquity,' says a French
writer;—but, as one may hope, with only partial
truth in the description ; for the Phoenicians
amassed indeed wealth untold, and secured a
monopoly in most of the markets of the world ;
but they drove hard bargains on the strength
of their monopoly ; they eked out their gains
by kidnapping and trafficking in slaves. Wher-
ever they appeared they were dreaded and
disliked, though, for business purposes, they were
indispensable. Unpleasant names are already
applied to them in the Homeric poems. This

was, perhaps, partly due to the instinctive antipathy which has always existed between the Semitic and Aryan races. In part it may be traced to some inevitable misunderstanding between people who refuse to learn one another's language. But, making all allowance for these facts, and speaking without any anti-Semitic prejudice, we must own that the Phoenicians were an inhuman and unlovable race. They were animated by one passion, the greed of gain. Wealth was with them the end of life, and not the means. Theirs was, in Bacon's phrase, 'the sabbathless pursuit of fortune.' They had no larger horizons, no hopes beyond material advancement. Every artifice of concealment was employed by them to maintain their monopoly. With jealous exclusiveness they guarded the secret of their geographical discoveries, of their trade routes, of the winds and currents. By inventing fabulous horrors they sought to deter rivals from following in their track, and at times committed acts of murderous cruelty upon those whose indiscreet curiosity impelled them to pursue the quest.

To the past and the future they were alike indifferent. Among the articles of their export trade we may reckon the alphabet, through which they conveyed to Greece the art of writing, though they themselves never really learnt to write. Enough for them if they could draw up their tariffs and keep their accounts. Even of their own history they have left no records; and it is to the research of the Greeks that we are almost wholly indebted for such fragments of information as we possess. Literature they had none. Their art was merely an imitation or reminiscence of the art of others. The sense of political unity, again, was wanting; for Phoenicia was not a country or a continuous territory, but a series of ports. Their municipal life was not without the vigour which is often inspired by commercial activity; and, on occasion, too, Phoenician towns displayed heroic qualities in defending their independence. But, speaking roughly, we may say that civic discipline and loyalty were but feebly felt; even the great colony of Carthage suffered the battles of the State to be

fought mainly by mercenaries.   In the absence
of any high ideal of personal or national welfare
the individual was crushed in the onward
movement of material civilisation.

Let us turn now to Greece.   The Greeks,
also, were born sailors and traders, who from the
dawn of history looked upon the sea as their
natural highway, and explored its paths in a
spirit in which the love of science and the love
of adventure were equally blended.   To them
might be applied the name, 'Αειναῦται,[1] which
was given to a party of shipowners at Miletus
who transacted their business on board ship.
They too were always afloat—their home was
on the sea.   Like the Phoenicians, they were
shrewd men of business, keen in the pursuit of
commerce, eager to make money.   From the
Phoenicians they learned all the arts and handi-
crafts ; by degrees they wrested from them the
secrets of their trade routes, and equipped
themselves with all the instruments of wealth
and civilisation which their jealous teachers
sought to retain in their own hands.   But with

[1] Plutarch ii. 298 c.

E

the Greeks the love of knowledge was stronger
than any instinct of monopoly; the love of
knowledge carried with it the desire to impart
it, and in giving to others they received again
their own with usury.   No people was ever less
detached from the practical affairs of life, less
insensible to outward utility; yet they regarded
prosperity as a means, never as an end.   The
unquiet spirit of gain did not take possession of
their souls.   Shrewd traders and merchants,
they were yet idealists.   They did not lose
sight of the higher and distinctively human
aims which give life its significance.   They had
a standard of measure, a faculty of distinguishing values; the several elements of national
welfare fell each into its proper place and
order.   The Greek states did not, it is true,
all in equal measure grasp the principle of the
subordination of the lower to the higher aim.
In Corinth and Aegina, where the Semitic
instinct for trade was dominant, the distinction
between the material means and the moral or
intellectual ends was not apprehended with the
same sureness or so decisively translated into

action as at Athens.   Still the fact remains
that Greece was aware of the ideal ends of life ;
Phoenicia was not.   And so political science,
ignored by the Phoenicians, became to the
Greeks the highest of the practical sciences,
the science of man, not as a trader, but as a
man, fulfilling his function as a member of the
social organism, and living with all the fulness
of life.   Aristotle speaks of the State as existing not 'for the sake of mere life, but of the
noble life ' ; and, though the formula is his own
and bears a philosophic stamp, he was but
following the guidance of educated thought and
deepening a popular conviction.   Granted that
certain external conditions must be satisfied
and material wants supplied, the true aim of
civic existence still lies beyond.   The State
was felt to be no mere mechanism for the
getting of wealth ; its function was to build up
character and intellect, to unfold the powers of
the heart as well as of the head, to provide free
scope for the exercise of human personality in
its manifold activities.   An Athenian could
have said with Burke : ' The State is a partner-

ship in all science, in all art, in every virtue,
and in all perfection.' The Greek orators are
animated by the same conception. Demosthenes never wearies of insisting on the moral
basis of national greatness. Wealth, population,
armies, fleets, all the material elements of
strength, if disjoined from the nobler sources of
civic inspiration, become 'useless, ineffectual,
unavailing.' [1]

Phoenicia remains a lasting witness to the
instability of power resting on a purely
commercial basis and unsustained by any lofty
or aspiring aims. No more striking contrast
can be drawn than that between Greek and
Phoenician colonisation. From the Phoenicians
the Greeks learnt all the rudiments of the
colonising art. But the Phoenician colonies,
scattered over the Mediterranean shores, were
as a rule little more than trading stations and
factories planted along the great international
routes; paying over, in some cases, to the
mother city a portion of their commercial
revenues, but owning no real allegiance, and not

[1] *Phil.* iii. 40 ἄχρηστα, ἄπρακτα, ἀνόνητα.

infrequently detached in sentiment. Nor did
they show much power of self-government or
any aptitude for entering into political union
with others. To keep on good terms with the
native populations on whose land they had
settled, and to turn to profitable use the
resources of the neighbouring tribes, was their
chief endeavour. Carthage, indeed, the greatest
of Phoenician colonies, displayed a magnificent
and conquering energy ; but her projects of
territorial ambition in Sicily, Sardinia, and
Spain were precisely the occasion of her downfall.

The influence of Greater Greece is the
determining fact in the history of the Hellenic
people. Already in the sixth century B.C. the
coasts and islands were studded with Greek
towns from the Crimea to North Africa, from the
regions of the Caucasus to Lower Italy, to Sicily,
and even to Gaul. In the Macedonian period
the chain of Greek cities extended to the Indus.
Plato might speak of the sea as 'a bitter and
brackish neighbour,'[1] a pleasant thing enough

[1] *Laws* iv. 705 A ἀλμυρὸν καὶ πικρὸν γειτόνημα.

to have near you, but dangerous, and likely to bring in other strange products besides foreign merchandise.　Nature, however, had marked out a maritime destiny for the Hellenes, and their colonial activity was the highest political achievement of the race.　Different motives led the several states to send out colonies.　Greece was a poor country—πενίη ἀεί κοτε σύντροφός ἐστι:[1]—the growth of population outstripped the means of existence, and a foreign market was necessary to supplement the food supply and to furnish the material for native industries. But though actual need was perhaps the most frequent of the impelling causes of emigration, the highest instincts of the race sought other satisfaction in the colonising energy.　Each founding of a city was a missionary enterprise. The emigrants carried with them the Apolline worship as the symbol of their spiritual unity ; and, as we expressly read in regard to the founding of Naxos (735 B.C.)—the earliest of the Greek colonies in Sicily—the first act on touching the new shore was to erect an altar to Apollo

[1] Herod. vii. 102.

Archegetes.[1] The jealousies which were so rife
in the narrow cantons of Greece were softened
and sometimes forgotten in absence from home.
The sense of Hellenic kinship was deepened
and clarified. The Hellenes became aware of
themselves as children of one family, however
widely dispersed ; guardians of a common heritage which they were bound to protect against
surrounding barbarism ; they listened to one
Homer, they were nurtured on the same heroic
legends ; on the same days they sacrificed to
the same gods as their kinsfolk in the mother
cities ; they lived under customs and institutions
similar in spirit to the old.

Great diversity of aim and method prevailed
in the colonising states. Corinth, the Venice
of antiquity, pursued a commercial policy, and
that policy rested on a colonial basis. Athens,
entering much later on the field of colonial
expansion, kept larger political and social ends
in view. Her colonial empire, growing out of a
religious federal union, owed its final and distinctive form to the part the city played in repelling

---

[1] Thucyd. vii. 3. 1.

the common danger which menaced Greece
during the Persian wars. Even into the work
of colonisation Athens sought to introduce a
large and comprehensive spirit. A salient
example occurs in the history of Magna
Graecia, the home of so many novel and interesting experiments in social organisation.
After the destruction of Sybaris, the new city
(henceforth named Thurii) was restored under
the guidance of Pericles, who desired to make
it a Panhellenic community : from the outset
it comprised not Athenians only but Arcadians,
Eleans, and Boeotians. But widely as the
states of Greece differed as colonising agencies,
Hellenic colonisation, viewed generally, had one
notable characteristic. Fitting in with the
spirit of adventure and the disinterested curiosity of a restless and daring intellect, it carried
men into the heart of every science. With the
enlargement of the physical horizon new intellectual needs sprang up. The art of navigation demanded a closer study of astronomy and
mathematics. The opening up of unknown
lands, the importation of unfamiliar products,

the acquaintance gained with alien civilisations, whetted the desire for anthropological and historical research. We can observe the fascinating influence of geographical discoveries on the imagination of a poet such as Aeschylus. We are reminded of the effect of similar explorations on our own Elizabethan age. Indeed, the versatile colonial intellect of Greece, with its many-sided and, as it might seem, incompatible activities, produced a type of character which it is not too fanciful to compare with so romantic a personality as that of Sir Walter Raleigh, who was 'poet, historian, chemist, soldier, philosopher, courtier.'

The intellectual movement of the Greek world during the sixth century, and down to about the middle of the fifth century, radiates from Greater Greece. The philosophic intellect of Ionia led the way. All the early philosophers are Ionians by birth—Thales, Anaximander, Anaximenes, Anaxagoras, Pythagoras, Xenophanes, Heraclitus ; and of these the first three belong to one city Miletus. That same Miletus, which from the eighth century onwards sent forth intrepid mariners, who penetrated to the remotest corners of the Euxine, planting some eighty settlements along the 'inhospitable' shores, also made fearless excursions into the domain of physical science, and gave to western Europe its first speculative impulse. In philosophy, the colonies of Southern Italy and Sicily followed the Ionian lead. In poetry, the earliest outburst of inspired song after Homer came from the island of Lesbos. Sicily gave birth to comedy, to dramatic dialogue, to rhetoric. The smaller islands contributed their share. Ceos produced the great Simonides ; Samos, Pythagoras ; Cos, Hippocrates, the father of medicine ; a century later Crete gave to the world the Cynic Diogenes ; and Melos, the 'atheist' Diagoras. Withdraw from Greece the colonies of her own blood, and you rob her of some of her greatest names ; not only those just mentioned, but also Terpander, Archilochus, Mimnermus, Arion, Alcaeus, Sappho, Stesichorus, Anacreon, Ibycus, Bacchylides, Epicharmus, Empedocles, Herodotus, Hellanicus, Gorgias—I need not complete the list.

In the colonies again the most diverse
political experiments were tried. The old
forms of constitution proved to be too rigid
for the new countries. Difficult problems presented themselves and pressed for practical
solution. All the adaptive powers of the race,
their rich and flexible intelligence, their εὐτρα-
πελία, were called into play. Rival centres of
industry or culture each acquired a distinctive
character. The literature, the art, the mode of
thought of the several colonies took their own
local colouring. The marvel is that at a dis-
tance from home, a mere handful of strangers,
they were not merged in the prevailing barbarism ; that they did not 'forget their language,
forget their poets, and their gods.'[1] As it was,
they not only maintained their Hellenism de-
spite all diversity of developments, but enriched
the common stock by a ceaseless output of ideas.
The sacred fire taken from the hearth of the
metropolis city, they kept alive, and from it
kindled new and illuminating thoughts which
they transmitted to the land of their origin.

[1] Perrot, *Histoire de l'Art dans l'Antiquité*, vii. 299.

The history of Greek art[1] offers multiplied
instances of this vital and effective interaction
between the colonies and the mother city. A
colony, free from the hampering traditions of a
school, aided, it might be, by the discovery of a
new material as the medium of artistic expression,
would strike out some bold experiment which
only received its finished form in the old home.
Among the causes which acted as a powerful
stimulus on artistic production none ranks
higher than the agonistic contests of Greece.
The desire to win national renown in this field
of coveted achievement created a civic rivalry,
intense in character and of far-reaching consequence. Each state was eager to know and
appropriate the best results that had elsewhere
been accomplished. Hence there was an un-
limited interchange of art products extending
even to the outlying regions of Hellenism.
Famous artists travelled with their wares. Not
only were the great religious and social centres,
such as Olympia, Delphi, Delos, Miletus reposi-

---

[1] Here I am much indebted to hints kindly given me by
Professor Waldstein.

tories—we might almost say museums—where
works of art could be viewed, but minor localities also took a pride in acquiring masterpieces
representing well-known individuals or different
schools. This free trade in art had in it an
educative and expansive force; it gave unity
no less than variety to artistic culture; it
quickened the sense of Hellenic patriotism; it
had an influence analogous to that exercised by
the poetic recitations of the wandering rhap-
sodists on the thought, the language, and the
sentiment of Greece.

Here I can do no more than allude to the
topic. For the detail we should recall the
history of sculpture from the second half of the
seventh century onward, especially in connexion with Chios, Crete, Samos, and other islands,
whence the hereditary craft of certain families
and schools found its way to the Grecian main-
land. To Glaucus of Chios is attributed the
invention of soldering iron; to Melas of Chios,
the first working of marble—an art which he
bequeathed to his son Micciades and his direct
descendants, Archermus, Bupalus, and Athennis.

In Samos the art of bronze-casting originated with Rhoecus and his son Theodorus. Crete produced a well-known school of sculpture, the earliest names being those of Dipoenus and Scyllis, who travelled through Greece proper, visiting Sicyon, Argos, Cleonae, and Ambracia, and there introduced their new methods. Later, during the second half of the sixth century and the first half of the fifth, we note the fresh and daring originality displayed in sculpture by Sicily—pre-eminently in the earlier metopes from Selinus—and also by Magna Graecia. Pythagoras of Rhegium, a rival of Myron of Eleutherae, and famous chiefly as the sculptor of Olympic victors, introduced his principles of 'symmetry and rhythm'; he marks the last step in the process of emancipation from archaic and hieratic bonds, which prepared the way for the age of Phidias. Another colonial sculptor of genius was a contemporary of Phidias—Paeonius of Mende, near Aenus in the Thracian Chersonese. His *Nike*, discovered at Olympia in 1875, exhibits an original spirit which undoubtedly influenced the art of the fifth century.

Again, in painting, Polygnotus of Thasos, under whom were executed the great mural decorations at Athens, appears to have held with Cimon a position similar to that of Phidias with Pericles. In the Periclean age itself one of the most distinctive features of Attic art is its breadth of view, its large hospitality, its power of assimilating every fruitful element of artistic taste and culture which came to it from all other Hellenic centres. Even in the following period, when Argos and Sicyon and Athens took the lead, it is worth remembering that among sculptors Scopas was a Parian ; and in the fourth century, when painting reached its highest point, the masters of the art were Zeuxis from Heraclea, Parrhasius from Ephesus, and Apelles from Colophon.

In that enchanted island of Sicily, which for more than a thousand years was the battle-ground of southern Europe, swept by a long succession of conquering races, Greeks and Phoenicians confronted one another for centuries. At certain critical moments of history Phoenicia threatened to engulf our Western civilisation.

Yet to-day, go where we may through the island, it is Greece that speaks to us, in her theatres and temples, in her ruined columns and along deserted shores. The voice of Greek poets, Greek philosophers and historians, who lived or died there, is still heard in the undying pages of the past. As for Phoenicia, in Sicily as elsewhere, her memorial has perished with her. In her day she did some humble, but real, service to mankind in helping forward, though with a reluctant hand, a more gifted people on the road of material progress. To her they owed their first lessons in shipbuilding and navigation, their knowledge of some of the lesser arts and crafts, and, as it would seem, certain practical applications of arithmetic. But, with all her wealth, she passed away, as was foretold by Ezekiel in his doom of Tyre, and the vestiges of her that remain have an antiquarian, not a human interest.

It is just this human quality, lacking in the Phoenicians, which marks so conspicuously the Hellenic temperament. There is in it a natural expansiveness, a desire to enter into kindly human relations with others, to exchange greetings with the stranger on the road, to give utterance to the passing thought or fugitive emotion ; or, if oral utterance is impossible, to make writing serve the turn of speech, and so bind together in friendly intimacy the present and the absent, the living and the dead.   Even inanimate objects are drawn into the circle of this genial human intercourse.   A bowl fore-stalls your curiosity by telling you something of its personal history.   A word or jotting on a piece of pottery—sometimes a mere "προσ-αγορεύω"—carries the message of the artist to his friend.   Or again, a fragment inscribed with the name of an Athenian youth calls up a tender reminiscence of old friendship when it is found far from Athens in the rock-tombs of Etruria.   The "χαῖρε," again, that is uttered over the departed is repeated on the sepulchral slab ; and not infrequently the farewell word is expanded into a brief dialogue between the dead man and the surviving friend, or even a chance wayfarer.   Such sepulchral greetings have a memorial value of a very special kind.

F

Unlike more formal monumental inscriptions, they are the direct address of person to person ; they make an immediate appeal to the heart for the very reason that they are so simple, so spontaneous ; as if the unspoken thought had been intercepted before it reached the lips, and had taken external shape while yet upon its way.

In all these instances mind is not subjected to things material ; it is the inner world that dominates the outward. This is of a piece with other characteristics already noted. In Plato's ideal commonwealth material well-being does not occupy a commanding place. The true constituent elements of happiness are moral and intellectual. It is only in the Utopias of the comic poets that material enjoyments come into the foreground of the picture. In one of the fragments of Pherecrates [1] (a contemporary of Aristophanes), human beings are by the bounty of Plutus equipped with all good things without any effort of their own : 'Of their own accord rivers of black broth,

---

[1] *ap*. Athen. vi. 97.

gushing and gurgling, will flow along the high-
ways from the springs of Plutus. . . . From
the roofs rivulets will run of the juice of the
grape with cheese-cakes and hot soup and
omelets made of lilies and anemones.' Some
rabbinical descriptions of the material happiness
that will prevail in the visible kingdom of God
do not fall far short of this comic paradise.
The rivers will flow with wine and honey ; the
trees will grow bread and delicacies ; in certain
districts springs will break forth which will
cure all diseases ; suffering will cease, and men
will be very long-lived, if they die at all. Even
if we admit that 'a good dose of materialism
may be necessary for religion that we may not
starve the world,' still Judaism, even in its
loftiest moments, is a little too much inclined
to hanker after material delights, and to express
itself in a form which would have shocked the
ideal sentiment of Greece. Take again the
enjoyment of a Greek festival. The occasion
was not, as with other nations, one for eating
and drinking. The people shared the more
refined tastes of their gods, who, at the agonistic

and dramatic festivals, came forth for the day
from their sanctuaries, and mingled gladly
with the throng of worshippers, demanding
from them no costly banquets, but perfected
human powers dedicated to the service of
religion : physical manhood with all its disciplined skill ; powers too of intellect and
imagination, expressing themselves in diverse
forms of poetry and music. Similarly in the
great national athletic contests, so long as the
finer instinct of Greece prevailed over Asiatic
ostentation, the reward of the victor had
no material value ; the wreath of wild olive,
laurel, or parsley, with which he was crowned,
was but the symbol of his consecration, nor
did he retain it as a personal possession ; it
was hung up in the shrine of the local deity.

The Greek way of regarding private luxury
offers a similar note of idealism. Money
lavished on purely personal enjoyment was
counted vulgar, oriental, inhuman. It was an
offence against good taste, a violation of the
law of measure and self-restraint, the glorifica-
tion of the individual on his selfish side. It

implied a failure to discern the true ends which make social existence desirable. The famous saying of Pericles, 'We are lovers of the beautiful, but without extravagance' (φιλοκα-λοῦμεν γὰρ μετ' εὐτελείας), may be taken as the motto of the private life of the Periclean agè. Refinement and simplicity—such was the ideal union. Mere economy had no attraction for a Greek, the real question being not the amount you spend, but the occasion of the outlay and the end in view. As for meanness, it was viewed with special disfavour. We may recall the man in Aristotle's *Ethics*, who, having spent liberally on a fitting object, then spoils the whole effect for the sake of a trifle (ἐν μικρῷ τὸ καλὸν ἀπολεῖ).[1] But, of all forms of meanness, the worst was that which was combined with display ; of which we have an example in a fragment of a comic poet, where an economical person boasts that he had invited his guests to a wedding breakfast on the express understand-ing that they were each to bring their own food. Large outlay on rare and interesting occasions

---

[1] *Eth. Nic.* iv. 2. 21.

even in private life meets with approval from
Aristotle ; and one of the most characteristically
Greek features in his description of such justifi-
able outlay is that not only is the outlay on the
great scale, it is also in the grand manner.
The total effect is impressive ; it depends not
on the amount expended, but on a certain
harmonious and aesthetic quality that affects
the imagination.[1]

Great outlay, according to the old ideal of
Athens, should be limited to public objects.
In the next generation, Demosthenes looks back
with regret to the lost simplicity of private life.
In earlier Athens, he says, the houses of
Miltiades and Themistocles differed in no way
from those of the ordinary citizen, while the
public buildings and temples were on a scale of
grandeur and magnificence that no future ages
could surpass.[2] The vast sums spent on the
Parthenon and other edifices have, indeed, been
criticised by some modern economists as so
much wealth locked up in bricks and mortar—
as unproductive expenditure which contributed

[1] *Eth. Nic.* iv. 2. 10.   [2] Dem. *Olynth.* iii. 25-26.

to the ruin of Athens. From the narrow
financial point of view it may be difficult to
justify such expenditure. But, if we try to look
at it in the Athenian spirit, is there not much
to be said in its defence? Simplicity in the
home, splendour in the city—that was the
principle. To spend largely on our private
selves, on our personal satisfaction, was luxury,
and culpable luxury. To incur great outlay
for worthy objects which transcend self and
minister to the enjoyment of the community,
was praiseworthy munificence. The individual
man and his material surroundings passed away;
the city was the enduring reality; it was in
some sense a spiritual fabric, the embodiment
of the people's nobler aspirations, of their higher,
their collective self. All the efforts of art might
worthily be expended in its service; that wealth
was not wasted which added to its beauty and
dignity, and inspired in the citizens a passionate
and admiring attachment. Here, again, the
Athenians look beyond material interest or profit,
and estimate the value of a thing in relation to
ideal ends, which are above the world of sense.

This conviction that the things of the mind have a worth, an inherent dignity, which cannot be measured in terms of money, is at the root of many Greek ideas on education. If we would pursue knowledge aright, we must love it disinterestedly. Even learning may be followed in the spirit of a shopkeeper ; and the intellectual vulgarity thus fostered is more ignoble than the frank avowal of money-getting as in itself the end. Nothing is so truly degrading as the intrusion of lower and mercenary motives into the sphere of the higher activities. Plato[1] distinguishes between the education which aims only at outward and worldly success and the true, the liberal education, which fits men for perfect citizenship. ' We are not now speaking of education in the narrower sense, but of that other education in virtue from youth upwards, which makes a man eagerly pursue the ideal perfection of citizenship, and teaches him how rightly to rule and how to obey. This is the only education which, upon our view, deserves the name ; that other sort of training

---

[1] *Laws* i. 643 F–644 A.

which aims at the acquisition of wealth or
bodily strength, or mere cleverness apart from
intelligence and justice, is mean and illiberal,
and is not worthy to be called education
at all.'

The superior value of leisure in the Hellenic
scheme of life as compared with work connects
itself with this high ideal of citizenship.   Leisure
is the Hellenic starting-point, the normal condition of the citizen, the prerogative of freemen.
Without leisure there is no freedom.   'We
work,' says Aristotle, 'in order that we may
have leisure.'[1]   At first sight this may bear
some resemblance to the schoolboy view of the
working term as being of the nature of an
interruption, an infelicitous break, in the holi-
days.   But leisure to the Greek thinker means
not the opposite of activity—for activity is of
the essence of life—but a special form of
activity ; an activity not evoked by external
needs, but free, spontaneous, and delightful ; an
ordered energy which stimulates all the vital
and mental powers.   It is an energy strenuous

---

[1] *Nic. Eth.* x. 7. 6 ἀσχολούμεθα γὰρ ἵνα σχολάζωμεν.

and productive, released from the bondage of
mechanical routine, and satisfying at once the
instinct for conduct, the instinct for knowledge,
and the instinct for beauty. Hence the
organised enjoyment of leisure was elevated by
the Greeks into a national art, and associated
with religion and politics. The games, the
festivals, the dramatic performances provided
the community with a refined recreation which
was the birthright and privilege of all. Greek
leisure, then, was not idleness. With the more
finely endowed natures it led to philosophy.
There is a passage in Plato's *Symposium* [1] where
Apollodorus, a pupil of Socrates, is speaking of
his love of philosophic conversation. 'But
when I hear other discourses, especially those
of rich men and traders, they are irksome to
me. I pity you who are my companions, because you always think that you are hard at
work when you are really doing nothing'
(οἴεσθέ τι ποιεῖν οὐδὲν ποιοῦντες). So the mere
money-maker is the idler; it is he who is
engaged in unproductive labour. The 'lover

[1] *Symp.* 173 C.

of wisdom' is the true worker ; he consecrates
his leisure to ends that are human and delightful.   It is half playfully said, but one sees the
meaning.   And it reminds one a little of a passage
in R. L. Stevenson's *Inland Voyage*, where he
tells of the evening he spent at the Club-house
of the *Royal Sport Nautique* in Brussels.   'We
are all employed in commerce during the day ;
but in the evening, *voyez-vous, nous sommes
sérieux !* '   'These,' says Stevenson, 'were the
words.   They were all employed over the
frivolous mercantile concerns of Belgium during
the day ; but in the evening they found some
hours for the serious concerns of life.   I may
have a wrong idea of wisdom, but I think that
was a very wise remark.'   It was only in the
decay of civic life, when thought was divorced
from action, and cloistered learning had become
the fashion of a few, that σχολή or leisure came
to denote a busy trifling, and the adjective
' scholastic ' was accepted as equivalent to
' pedantic.'

With the ideal view of leisure went a corresponding ideal conception of friendship.   The

intellectual employment of leisure consisted
mainly in oral discussion on the deeper problems
of human life.   Only through the strife of conversation and the kindling contact of mind with
mind could truth be elicited.   An atmosphere
of intimacy was the first condition of disinterested learning.   Friendship and philosophy
were linked together in inseparable union, and
perfect friendship became in itself a mode of
mental illumination.   A man's 'wits and
understanding,' says Bacon, 'do clarify and
break up in the communicating and discoursing
with another.'   Friendship 'maketh daylight
in the understanding out of darkness and
confusion of thoughts.'   That is a genuine
Hellenic sentiment.   The friendships of Greece
are still proverbial ; and so important a factor
did   friendship   form   in   social   intercourse,
especially when the loss of freedom had robbed
politics of its chief interest, that the rules to be
found in the later Greek writers for the making
of friends are as numerous as the modern
prescriptions for making happy marriages.
Such phrases as 'he who has friends has no

friend ' [1] point to the high demands implied in
perfect friendship. The friendship between
good men as sketched by Aristotle [2] glows with
an eloquence which surprises us in a writer so
studiously quiet in tone, and deserves to stand
beside the impassioned chapter describing the
bliss of philosophic speculation. Friendship, he
tells us, is realised in that partnership of speech
and thought in which the distinctive life of man
consists, a life that is social, not merely
gregarious—'that is what living together
means ; it is not as with cattle herding on the
same spot.' To know that you have a good
man as your friend quickens the play of vital
energy ; it promotes the vivid consciousness of
life which is the essence of happiness. Your
friend is different from you and yet identified
with you ; and in the spectacle of his noble
actions and the sympathetic sense of his existence
your own sense of personality is ennobled. It
is even a friend's privilege to give up wealth,

---

[1] Diog. Laert. v. 21 ᾧ φίλοι οὐδεὶς φίλος. So *Eth. Eud.*
1245 b 20 οὐδεὶς φίλος ᾧ πολλοὶ φίλοι.

[2] *Eth. Nic.* ix. ch. 8 and 9.

station, life itself, for the sake of his friend, and
so achieve the true self-love, realising his higher
self through self-sacrifice. 'He will prefer,'
says Aristotle, 'the intense joy of a brief
moment to the feeble satisfaction of an age,
one glorious year of life to many years of trivial
existence, one great and glorious deed to many
insignificant actions.'[1]   Friendship is for Aristotle the glorified form of human intercourse.

I am far from suggesting that these Greek
ideals, just as they stand, can be transferred to
our own age and country.   In many points of
detail the Greek way cannot be our way.
Some lines of necessary divergence will at once
have occurred to you while I have been speaking.   Under the stress of our industrial life
the principles here indicated will need adjustment, adaptation, limitation.   But the principles
themselves, I would submit, are profoundly and
permanently true.   And, in the task of education,
perhaps, as much as in any department of civic

---

[1] *Eth. Nic.* ch. 9. 9 ὀλίγον γὰρ χρόνον ἡσθῆναι σφόδρα μᾶλλον
ἕλοιτ' ἂν ἢ πολὺν ἠρέμα, καὶ βιῶσαι καλῶς ἐνιαυτὸν ἢ πόλλ' ἔτη
τυχόντως, καὶ μίαν πρᾶξιν καλὴν καὶ μεγάλην ἢ πολλὰς καὶ
μικράς.

life, we need a reminder that there are certain ideals of character, certain paramount ends of conduct, which should underlie and determine all our efforts. We are tempted, perhaps, to fix our eyes on the machinery of education, on the subjects of instruction, on the direct mercantile results of our system, on our own immediate ends as the teachers of this or that branch of knowledge. But sometimes we may do well to test and revise our standards ; to ask ourselves what, after all, we are aiming at, what kind of human being we desire to produce.

It was part of the beneficent function of Greece to emphasise this idea. The Greeks, as I have tried to show, introduced a large and humanising conception into the one-sidedness of an earlier civilisation with which they came in contact. They had a perception of what Isaiah calls 'the things by which men live.' They knew that 'man does not live by bread alone,' that livelihood is not life, that mere wealth is not well-being. The satisfaction of material wants is not the end of human endeavour. The wealth of nations, like the happiness of individuals, has its source deeper than in the accumulation of riches or the expansion of commerce.   The true value of the goods of life is determined by the sense of life as a whole, and by their relation to the higher and distinctively human ends of existence.   All this may be called idealism.   I have here omitted all reference to the ideal creations of Greek poetry, to those features of character which lift the men and women of Homer or Sophocles above the trivial and the real, and which, in spite of all moral flaws and imperfections, make us feel that they belong to a humanity nobler and richer than the people of our everyday world— that they are real and concrete personalities, and yet ideal types.   Nor, again, have I mentioned the heroic figures who stand out at intervals in the pages of Greek history—men who responded to great calls of duty and showed a splendid disregard of consequences ; rare and exceptional men such as inspired the biographies of Plutarch. I speak of idealism in a more restricted sense.   We have seen how the breath of poetry touches the common affairs of life, disengaging the things of the mind from the things of sense. It is partly poetry, partly philosophy ; for the Hellenic people felt by a poetic instinct truths which their philosophers arrived at by reflection and analysis. It was these truths that gave meaning and reality to the public and private life of the Greeks—their institutions, their external surroundings, their recreations—to their estimate of human personality and human fellowship, so that the practical world was for them lit up by an imaginative ideal.

III

THE GREEK LOVE OF KNOWLEDGE

No one can read Homer without being aware
that the spirit of man has here shaken off
the torpor of an earlier world and has asserted
its freedom. There is no brooding sense of
mystery ; none of those oppressive secrets with
which the atmosphere of Oriental poetry is
charged. A fresh and lucid intelligence looks
out upon the universe. There is the desire to
see each object as it is, to catch it in some
characteristic moment of grace or beauty. And
the thing seen is not felt to be truly understood
until it has taken shape in words, and the exact
impression conveyed to the eye has been transmitted to another mind. A single epithet, one
revealing word in Homer will often open up to
us the very heart of the object ; its inmost and

permanent character will stand out in clear-cut outline. Nothing is too great, nothing too trivial, to be worth describing—the sea, the dawn, the nightly heavens, the vineyard, the winter torrent, the piece of armour, the wool-basket, the brooch, the chasing on a bowl. Over each and all of these the poet lingers with manifest enjoyment. There is but a single exception to the rule of minute delineation. In the description of the human person the outward qualities are but lightly touched. Beauty and stature—these are noted in general terms ; the colour of the hair is sometimes added ; not unfrequently, it would seem, as a racial characteristic. But the portraiture of the individual is not drawn with any exactitude. There is no inventory of the features of men or of fair women, as there is in the Greek poets of the decline or in modern novels. Man is something different from a curious bit of workmanship that delights the eye. He is a 'speaker of words and a doer of deeds,' and his true delineation is in speech and action, in thought and emotion.

Again, though each thing, great and small, has its interest, the great and the small are not of equal importance. There is already a sense of relative values ; the critical spirit is awake. The *naïveté* of Homeric society must not lead us to think of Homer as representing rude and primitive thought. Homer stands out against a vast background of civilisation. The language itself is in the highest degree developed— flexible and expressive, with a fine play of particles conveying delicate shades of feeling, and suggestion. Homeric men are talkative ; each passing mood seeks some form of utterance ; but garrulous they are not. They wish to speak, but they have always something to say. They are bent on making their feelings and actions intelligible. They endeavour to present their case to themselves as it presents itself to the minds of others. They appeal both to living witnesses and to the experience of the past ; they compare and they contrast ; they bring the outer and the inner world into significant connexion ; they enforce their arguments by sayings containing the condensed wisdom of life. Homeric discourse, with the marvellous resources of its vocabulary, its structural coherence, its intimate union of reason and passion, has in it all the germs of future Greek oratory.

Moreover, the poet aims at being more than entertaining. He sings to an audience who desire to extend their knowledge of the facts of life, to be instructed in its lessons, to enlarge their outlook. Gladly they allow themselves to be carried into the region of the unknown. Common reality does not suffice. They crave for something beyond it. But the world of the imagination is no nebulous abode of fancy ; it is still the real world, though enriched and transfigured, and throbbing with an intenser life. Through known adventures they pass imperceptibly into an undiscovered country— strange and yet familiar—in which they still find themselves at home. Poetry is not for them, as it so often is for us, an escape from reality, a refuge from world-weariness.

Strabo observes that 'to construct an empty teratology or tale of marvels on no basis of truth is not Homeric ' ; [1] and that 'the *Odyssey* like the *Iliad* is a transference of actual events to the domain of poetry.' [2]

He insists, in particular, that 'the more Homeric critics' (οἱ Ὁμηρικώτεροι)—as opposed to Eratosthenes and his school—'following the poems verse by verse' (τοῖς ἔπεσιν ἀκολοθοῦντες) were aware that the geography of Homer is not invented ; that he is 'the leader of geographical knowledge' (ἀρχηγέτης τῆς γεωγραφικῆς ἐμπειρίας),[3] and that his stories are accurate, more accurate than those of later ages.[4] Strabo has, of course, an excessive belief in the scientific accuracy of Homer ; still the *Odyssey* is a truly remarkable geographical document, and recent investigations tend to heighten its value as a record of early travel. The desire indeed to identify Homeric localities and even personages, has

---

[1] Strabo i. 2. 9 ἐκ μηδενὸς δ' ἀληθοῦς ἀνάπτειν κενὴν τερατολογίαν οὐχ Ὁμηρικόν. Cp. i. 2. 17 τὸ δὲ πάντα πλάττειν οὐ πιθανόν, οὐδ' Ὁμηρικόν.

[2] *Ib.* iii. 2. 13 ὥστε καὶ τὴν Ὀδύσσειαν καθάπερ καὶ τὴν Ἰλιάδα ἀπὸ τῶν συμβάντων μεταγαγεῖν εἰς ποίησιν.

[3] *Ib.* i. 1. 2.   [4] *Ib.* i. 2. 7.

led to some strange results both in ancient and modern times. An ingenious writer, who has translated the *Odyssey*, convinced himself that the authoress of the poem was 'a very young woman who lived at a place now called Trapani, and introduced herself into the work under the name of Nausicaa'—the would-be princess being in truth a 'practised washerwoman,' who in several passages betrays a suspicious familiarity with that art. But, apart from such extravagances of criticism, the *Odyssey* in all its geographical bearings has lately been made the subject of a fascinating and exhaustive inquiry by M. Victor Bérard in his two volumes entitled, *Les Phéniciens et l'Odyssée*. Whatever may be thought of his Phoenician theories, and rash as we may regard some of his attempts at locating the scenes described in the poem, M. Bérard has shown with a wealth of illustrative material and under entirely new lights, how precise an acquaintance the poet had with the navigation of the Mediterranean, with its winds and currents, the coasts and islands, and with the habits of those early

mariners.[1]   Even when we pass into the outer
zone of the wanderings of Odysseus, there
are links of connexion with reality.   And we
can imagine with what avidity the seafaring
population of traders, pirates, and sailors on
their return home from their voyages listened
to the recitation of the *Odyssey*—to the
description of places lying on fabulous shores
or bordering on the world of fairyland, yet
calling up frequent reminiscences of the actual
lands they had themselves visited, and of perils
they had encountered.

The close correspondence in the *Odyssey*
between poetic fancy and the realities of a
mariner's life may be illustrated by a few
examples taken from M. Bérard.   In Book ii.
212 ff.[2] Telemachus asks the suitors for a
ship and twenty comrades, that he may go to
Sparta and sandy Pylos to inquire about his
father's return.   They refuse.   Athene, however, under the form of Mentor equips the

---

[1] Cp. Strabo i. 2. 20 κἀν τοῖς κλίμασι δὲ κἀν τοῖς ἀνέμοις
διαφαίνει τὸ πολυμαθὲς τὸ περὶ τὴν γεωγραφίαν Ὅμηρος.

[2] Bérard, vol. i. p. 64 ff.

expedition.   Some hours after sunset Mentor
and Telemachus set sail.   The time is marked
by line 388 :—

δύσετό τ' ἠέλιος σκιόωντό τε πᾶσαι ἀγυιαί—

a formula occurring, in connexion with travel,
seven times in the *Odyssey*, and denoting,
apparently, the dead of night.   Athene sent
them 'a favouring gale, a fresh wind from
the North West (ἀκραῆ Ζέφυρον) singing
over the wine-dark sea.'   Next morning at
dawn they reach Pylos.   Turn now to the
official 'Sailing Directions' of to-day.   In
these Greek waters, we are told, land and sea
breezes follow one another alternately.   The
sea breeze springs up each morning about 10
A.M.   During the day, therefore, it keeps the
ships locked in the harbour.   At sunset it falls.
Then for several hours there is a calm.   Towards 11 P.M. the land breeze rises.   Hence,
this ship of Telemachus leaving Ithaca about
11 P.M., sails almost before the wind to the
Peloponnese.   The wind and the pilot do the
work.   At early dawn the mariners easily make
the harbour.   Later, it would be more difficult,

for—see again 'Sailing Directions'—the land breeze then freshens, and does not fall till about 9 A.M. The poet who described this voyage of Telemachus wrote, we cannot doubt, with all the knowledge of a skipper.[1]

One more example may be added.[2]   In Book V. 295-296, after Odysseus had quitted the island of Calypso, as he approaches the Phaeacian coast a tempest arises :

σὺν δ' Εὖρός τε Νότος τε ἔπεσον Ζέφυρός τε δυσαὴς
καὶ Βορέης αἰθρηγενέτης μέγα κῦμα κυλίνδων.

'The South East and South West wind clashed and the stormy North West, and the North East that is born in the bright air, rolling onwards a great wave.' Here we have four winds, Eurus, Notus, Zephyrus, Boreas. Finally Boreas prevails (383-392). It lasts two days and two nights ; then it falls, and a

---

[1] The same custom of embarking at night is found in three other places in the *Odyssey* :—iv. 780 ff., where the sailors go to waylay Telemachus on his return ; xiii. 24 ff., describing the convoy of Odysseus from Phaeacia ; xv. 389 ff., Eumaeus' story of the Phoenician merchant-ship quitting the isle of Syria —the same formula being there used (xv. 471) as in ii. 388 δύσετό τ' ἠέλιος κ.τ.λ.

[2] Bérard, vol. i. p. 481 ff.

' windless calm' comes on. This was on the morning of the third day.

Again we look at our ' Sailing Directions.' ' It frequently happens,' we read, ' that winds from the N.E., N.W., and S.E. blow at the same time in different parts of the Adriatic. The wind called *Bora* is most to be feared and demands active and incessant watch. . . . Its most furious blasts are announced by the following symptoms — a black and compact cloud, surmounted by another cloud more light and fleecy, covers the horizon in the N.E. (cp. αἰθρηγενέτης). . . . In summer it never lasts more than three days.' [1]

This, says Bérard, is not the storm of literature, but a genuine Adriatic storm. Virgil's storms always last three days: that was part of his poetic furniture :

> Tres adeo incertos caeca caligine soles
> Erramus pelago, totidem sine sidere noctes.[2]

The poet of the *Odyssey* knows what he relates ; he is minutely accurate in each detail ; and the

---

[1] *Instructions Nautiques*, No. 706.
[2] *Aen.* iii. 203-204.

Adriatic storm, as he describes it, off the
Phaeacian coast, is a curious confirmation of
the old tradition that the island of Phaeacia is
none other than Corfu.

The love of knowledge (τὸ φιλομαθές), says
Plato,[1] is as marked a characteristic of the
Greeks as is the love of money (τὸ φιλοχρήμα-
τον) of the Phoenicians and Egyptians. From
the dawn of history *to know* seemed to the
Greeks to be in itself a good thing apart from
all results. They had a keen-eyed and disinterested curiosity for the facts of outward
nature, for man—his ways and his works—
for Greeks and Barbarians, for the laws and
institutions of other countries. They had the
traveller's mind, alert in observing and record-
ing every human invention and discovery. One
thing alone they viewed with unconcern—the
language of the foreigner. Up to the time of
Alexander, the Scythian Anacharsis is the only
traveller of whom we read as having thought it

---

[1] *Rep.* iv. 435 E. Cp. *Laws* v. 747 C, where the contrast
between σοφία and πανουργία is noted as a similar race distinction.

worth his while to learn any language other than his own. Neither Herodotus, nor Democritus, nor Plato, availed themselves, as far as we know, of any such linguistic aid in their researches. Greek seemed to them the only human language ; and even a sceptical philosopher like Epicurus felt no doubt that the gods, if they spoke at all, spoke in Greek. The neglect of foreign languages led to consequences more serious than the absurd etymological guesses that found acceptance in Greece. The notion that Greek words represented the original and natural names of things gave rise to mistaken theories as to the relation of language and thought. Even so great a thinker as Plato fell a victim to fallacies which could hardly have misled him had he been familiar with the grammar of any other tongue.

But the open eye and the open mind are not all that is required to discover truth. The Greeks soon became aware that, in order to see rightly, the facts must be looked for in a special way. 'The god of Delphi,' says Heraclitus, 'neither speaks nor conceals, but

gives a sign.'[1]   And again, 'Nature loves to
hide.'[2]   She must be tracked, therefore, into her
inmost recesses.   Her secret must be wrested
from her unawares.   In the process of initiation
into her mysteries no one can succeed who is
faint-hearted in the search.   'Unless a man has
good hope'—once more to quote Heraclitus—
'he shall not find out the unexpected.'[3]   Truth
assumes paradoxical forms.   It is the incredible
which happens, and the investigator must be
on the look-out for surprises.   But the stage of
wonder is only the initial stage in scientific
inquiry.   'We begin,' says Aristotle,[4] 'by
wondering that a thing should be so, just as
marionettes appear wonderful to those who
have not yet investigated the cause'; in the
end we should be astonished if things were not
as they are: 'there is nothing that would
astonish a geometrician more than if the

---

[1] Heracl. Fr. 11 [93] οὔτε λέγει οὔτε κρύπτει ἀλλὰ σημαίνει.

[2] *Ib.* 10 [123] φύσις κρύπτεσθαι φιλεῖ.

[3] *Ib.* 7 [18] ἐὰν μὴ ἔλπηαι, ἀνέλπιστον οὐκ ἐξευρήσει.

[4] Arist. *Met.* i. 2. 983 a 12-20. Cp. Plat. *Theaet.* p. 155 D
μάλα γὰρ φιλοσόφου τοῦτο τὸ πάθος, τὸ θαυμάζειν· οὐ γὰρ
ἄλλη ἀρχὴ φιλοσοφίας ἢ αὕτη.

diagonal should prove to be commensurate with the side.' The progress of science from the unexpected to the inevitable, as here described by Aristotle, is not unlike his account of the evolution of a dramatic action—the most impressive tragic effect being that which arises from the shock of surprise at an unlooked for event followed by the discovery of necessary sequence : the catastrophe, however startling, could not have been otherwise than it was : the end was already implicit in the beginning.[1]

From the outset Greek thinkers looked slightingly on that multifarious learning which holds together a mass of unrelated facts, but never reaches to the central truth of things. As soon as they began to think at all, they directed their energies to the search for causes, the discovery of law throughout the universe. They are tempted at times to be too much elated by their own successes, to accept a hasty generalisation, to be over-confident in the power of a formula ; they cannot decipher ' the long

[1] *Poet.* ix. 11 1452 a 2-3 (the union of the παρὰ τὴν δόξαν with the δι' ἄλληλα).

and difficult language of facts.'[1] Yet the facts
are looked at steadily, the data of experience are
interrogated, sifted, collated, by methods indeed
still imperfect, but without bias or partiality.
We can see the writers at their task, revising
and testing each judgment, and reviewing their
conclusions. What a refreshing candour, for
instance, it is when a physician, in one of the
Hippocratic writings (a treatise *On Diet in
Acute Diseases*) introduces a point he had over-
looked in the words, 'This argument will be of
assistance to my opponent.' Everywhere there
is the same invincible desire not to rest in outward appearances, but to penetrate to reality, to
interpret phenomena, to make the words of
nature and of man intelligible. Mere beliefs
or opinions—the image is that of Plato,[2] though
he shares the thought with many of his predecessors—are, like the statues of Daedalus,
runaway things : not until they have been tied
down by the chain of causal sequence do they

[1] Plat. *Polit*. 278 D τὰς τῶν πραγμάτων μακρὰς καὶ μὴ ῥᾳδίους
συλλαβάς.

[2] *Meno*, p. 97 E–98 A.

stand fast and become in the true sense knowledge. 'Rather,' said Democritus,[1] 'would I
discover the cause of one fact than become
King of the Persians.'

The love of knowledge worked on the Greeks
with a potent spell. It came to them as did
the Sirens' voice to Odysseus, luring him with
the promise that he should know all things—
the things that have been and those that are
to be.[2] They were, however, partly conscious
of the peril. And we find in them that the
spirit of inquiry, daring indeed and far-reaching, was generally combined with reverence.
It is not the timid Oriental fear that man might
find out too much and so incur the jealousy of
the gods—though of this feeling traces may be
detected ; chiefly, however, embedded in ancient
strata of mythology : it is a feeling rarely
hinted at in literature. The reverence I speak
of is rather that restraining instinct which
reminds man of the limits assigned to human

[1] Democr. ap. Eus. *Pr. Ev.* xiv. 27. 3 Δημόκριτος γοῦν αὐτὸς
ὥς φασιν ἔλεγε βούλεσθαι μᾶλλον μίαν εὑρεῖν αἰτιολογίαν ἢ τὴν
Περσῶν οἱ βασιλείαν γενέσθαι.

[2] *Odyss.* xii. 189-191.

H

faculties, and tells him that the utmost scope of his powers cannot avail completely to grasp the eternal order of the universe. Man cannot place himself at the centre and see as far as the circumference. Empedocles strikes this note in memorable verses : [1]

'Straitened are the powers that are shed through the limbs of men ; many the strange accidents that befal them, and blunt the edge of thought ; brief is the span of that life in death which they behold—swift death to which they are doomed ; then are they whirled away, and like a vapour fly aloft, each persuaded only of that on which he has himself chanced to light, driven this way and that. But the whole— man boasts that he has found it: all idly; for these things no eye hath seen, nor ear heard, neither may they be grasped by the mind. Thou, then, since thou hast strayed hither, shalt learn no more than human wisdom may discern. But, O ye gods, turn aside from my tongue the madness of these men. Hallow my lips and cause

---

[1] Emped. 36-49. In this passage some of the readings are doubtful.

to flow from them the stream of holy words.
And thee, I beseech, O Muse, much-wooed
maiden white-armed, tell me the things that the
creatures of a day may hear.   From the
House of Holiness speed me on my way and
guide thy willing car.'

As in conduct the pride (ὕβρις) which thrust
itself into a sphere not its own, and violated the
rights of others—gods or men—was condemned;
so too the feeling prevailed, though less
frequently asserted, that the intellect should
beware of over-stepping its proper limitations.
Here too it was right to exercise the quality of
temperate self-restraint (σωφροσύνη).   Take
again the magnificent opening lines of the poem
of Parmenides—the poet whose sight was
'straining straight at the rays of the sun.'[1]
The youthful inquirer is borne in the chariot of
thought to the house of the goddess Wisdom.
The daughters of the Sun show the way.   At
their entreaty the portals of the paths of night
and day are flung open by Retributive Justice
who holds the keys.   The goddess receives

[1] Parm. 144 αἰεὶ παπταίνουσα πρὸς αὐγὰς ἠελίοιο.

him graciously and proceeds to expound to him both truth and error—'the unshaken heart of persuasive truth' and the vain fancies of mortals. The reverential awe with which the search for Truth is here described is rare in the mouth either of poet or philosopher. But an ethical sense—a sense of moral limitations—akin to religious emotion, is conspicuous in the early Ionian philosophy. The great idea which Ionia contributed to human thought was that of the universal rule of law. It is one and the same law that runs through the physical and the moral world : 'The Sun will not overpass his bounds, or the Erinnyes, the ministers of justice, will find him out.' [1] The link is not yet broken between nature and man. The cosmic order rests on moral sanctions, on certain principles of limitation divinely ordained ; it is the embodiment of supreme Justice — that Justice whose earthly counterpart seemed to later Greek thinkers to stand at the summit of all the virtues :—'neither Evening nor Morning

[1] Heraclit. Fr. 29 [94] Ἥλιος οὐχ ὑπερβήσεται μέτρα· εἰ δὲ μή, Ἐρινύες μιν δίκης ἐπίκουροι ἐξευρήσουσι.

Star so wonderful.'[1]   The thought is not unlike
that of Wordsworth's lines :

> Thou dost preserve the stars from wrong ;
> And the most ancient heavens through Thee are fresh
> and strong.

Greek scientific knowledge, however, grew
up under secular influences, not as in the East
under the shadow of the temple.   There was
in Greece no separate and leisured class of
priests and scholars ; no sacred books which
hampered the free play of intellect.   Even
medicine, which is slow to detach itself from
magic, was developed in an atmosphere of lay-
thought, partly through the philosophic
investigation of nature, partly by the close
study of health and disease in those families of
physicians in which the art was hereditary.
Fortunately for the Greeks they were able to
utilise the scientific observations made in Egypt
and Chaldaea by an organised priesthood, while
they themselves dispensed with the teaching of

---

[1] Arist. *Nic. Eth.* v. I. 15 καὶ διὰ τοῦτο πολλάκις κράτιστος
τῶν ἀρετῶν εἶναι δοκεῖ ἡ δικαιοσύνη, καὶ οὔθ᾽ ἕσπερος οὔθ᾽ ἑῷος
οὕτω θαυμαστός.

the priests. All the accumulated lore of the earlier civilisations they appropriated, making it the starting-point for fresh inquiry. But they never rested in unverified tradition. Even religious cosmogonies they do not take ready-made. Science followed the ebb and flow of thought; its free movement was unhampered; its truths were not conveyed through hieratic channels and never hardened into lifeless dogmas.

Thus Greek science, Greek philosophy, is the awakening of the lay mind. The Greeks dared to ask the question ' Why ? ' The fact was not enough; they sought out the cause (τὸ διότι) behind the fact (τὸ ὅτι). Their answer to the ' Why ? ' is often wrong; but no anxious scruples, no priestly authority deterred them from venturing into the hidden domain of causes. In the abstract mathematical sciences they were the first to ask the *Why* of things, and seldom failed to hit on the true answer. One of the facts long known to Chinese, Hindoo, and Egyptian architects was that if the sides of a triangle are represented numerically by 3, 4, and 5, the sides whose lengths are 3 and 4, are

perpendicular to one another. Century upon
century passed before any one asked the
question, Why is this so? In a dialogue
written by a Chinese emperor, Tchaou-kong,
about 1100 B.C., in which the emperor himself
takes a part, his interlocutor reveals to him the
property of this famous triangle. ' Indeed !
wonderful ! ' exclaimed the emperor ; but it
never occurred to him to ask the reason :—
the wonder in which philosophy begins sometimes stops short of philosophy. Not till the
Greeks appeared in history was the reason
asked and the answer given. Greek geometry
was, in short, a new thing in the history of the
human mind. Geometry, according to Herodotus,
was born in Egypt ; but it was geometry as an
applied science, practical in its aims, and such
as was requisite for the arts of building and land-
surveying. Theoretic geometry the Greeks
created for themselves ; and so rapid was their
advance that by the fifth century B.C., as it
would seem, the greater part of what is contained in the elements of Euclid had attained
to demonstrative and logical form. The kind

of geometry which the Greeks discovered is characteristic of the idealist temperament so conspicuous in their art and literature. Lines which have length without breadth, which are absolutely straight or curved, indicate at once that we are in the region of pure thought. The conditions of empirical reality are neglected ; the mind is striving towards ideal forms. Pythagoras, we are told, offered a sacrifice to the gods in joy at a mathematical discovery. In what earlier civilisation was mathematics pursued with this disinterested ardour ?

The Jews as well as the Greeks felt that the paramount need of humanity was knowledge—that man should know the truth about himself and his relation to the power outside him. But the Greek, with unwearied insistence, asked himself, What is knowledge ? Can it be attained, and how ? No problem appeared to him more difficult. It was looked at from every side by a succession of great thinkers. Many and various were the answers. To the Jews, on the other hand, the answer was not remote or difficult ; there was but one knowledge and

that the highest : 'The word is very nigh unto
thee, in thy mouth and in thy heart, that thou
mayest do it.'   It had been revealed to them by
the divine voice; repeated at every crisis of
their marvellous history ; written indelibly on
the conscience of the nation ; it was indeed
the secret of which they were the repository, to
be guarded inviolate and disclosed in due time to
the world.   The knowledge of the Lord was
the beginning and end of wisdom.   And the
words of this wisdom—so ran the command—
'ye shall teach your children, speaking of them
when thou sittest in thine house, and when thou
walkest by the way, when thou liest down and
when thou risest up.   And thou shalt write them
upon the door-posts of thine house, and upon
thy gates.'

The Greeks, like the Jews, had their sacred
volume.   Already in the seventh century B.C.
at the Delian festival and in many other parts
of the Hellenic world, they assembled to hear
their minstrels recite the Homeric poems.   At
Athens, from the sixth century onward, a public
recitation of Homer was held every fourth year

at the Panathenaic festival. It was analogous to the Jewish provision that once in every seven years the law was to be read at the Feast of Tabernacles in the hearing of all Israel. In 444 B.C. we read of Ezra on his return from Babylon to Jerusalem renewing the old observance and reading the book of the law to the assembled people ; and it is curious to reflect that at Athens at the same time, in the Periclean era, the corresponding custom continued to exist. But there was this difference. Whereas for each nation, Jews and Greeks alike, the reading of their own ancient volume served to heighten the sense of spiritual kinship and to create an ideal of conduct : to the Greeks the Homeric poems had now become but one among many means of satisfying the needs of thought and imagination. The popular mind still found in them the knowledge of all things human and divine ; but the deeper and pressing intellectual problems that had arisen, met with no solution there. The drama was already presenting its own interpretations of human destiny ; philosophy had entered on its long quarrel with

poetry ; Socrates had started speculation on
the road that it was to pursue for centuries.
Received traditions were now being questioned.
The *Why* of duty, no less than the meaning of
knowledge, was being subjected to discussion.
Thus the Homeric poems, while they never
ceased to be the inspiration of the race, had lost
their unique authority.   Meanwhile to the Jews
the law, in the widest sense of the word, was
still the one book on which to meditate day and
night.   Nor was the knowledge of it a thing to
be received with languid or otiose mind, or in the
quietude of religious rapture.   Man's bliss was to
exercise himself therein, to go back upon it in his
inmost thoughts, to drink deeply of those inexhaustible springs.   The intervals of sacred leisure
which were enjoyed by all classes within the
community, were devoted to the deepening of
the religious life ; for the outward observance
of the Sabbath and the non-performance of
thirty-nine various kinds of work afterwards
enumerated by the Rabbis did not exhaust the
significance of the day to pious minds.   Moreover, as this knowledge was to be translated

into action, and adapted to all circumstances as the vivifying principle of conduct, it became necessary not to rest satisfied with the letter of the law, but to pass beyond the unwritten word, and divine the things that were unsaid,—or in the later Rabbinical phrase, 'the commands left to the human heart.' There remained a multitude of details outside the province of strict law, in which, as with the Greeks, the rules of conduct could only be discovered by immediate perception—by what Aristotle calls αἴσθησις—that delicate and sensitive faculty which intuitively apprehends the facts of the particular case.   Still the greater issues of life were once for all determined, and there was no riddle left for the wise man to solve.

Aristotle, like the Jew, places the supreme bliss of man in a certain mode of knowing and thinking.   But the human Reason is with him the one instrument by which this highest knowledge is to be attained.   It is a thing either intrinsically divine or the divinest gift that we possess.   Alone it is loved for its own sake ; of all our activities it is the most continuous, the most pleasurable, the least dependent on external conditions.   Man's felicity consists in the exercise of this sovereign faculty with such untiring vigour as our human condition admits. Such a life of speculation is the noblest employment of leisure.   It is an energy which is also tranquillity, an activity of mind that is set free from mechanical occupations and the pressure of material needs, and directed inward, not upon ends external to itself;—the deep repose of the soul in the contemplation of truth.   It is a life higher than human ; nor can we live it save in virtue of the divine principle inherent in us. ' Let us not listen therefore to those who tell us that as men and mortals we should mind only the things of man and of mortality ; but, so far as we may, we should bear ourselves as immortals (ἀθανατίζειν), and do all that in us lies to live in accord with that element within us, that sovereign principle of Reason, which is our true self, and which in capacity and dignity stands supreme.'[1]   Here we have the love of knowledge in its highest Greek conception,

---

[1] Arist. *Nic. Eth.* x. 7. 8 : see the whole chapter.

touched with religious emotion, and almost
carried into the sphere of mysticism. I need
not stay to enlarge on the divergence between
this ideal and that suggested by the words of
the Hebrew prophet : ' Let not the wise man
glory in his wisdom, neither let the mighty man
glory in his might . . . : but let him that glorieth
glory in this, that he understandeth and knoweth
me, that I am the Lord which exercise loving-
kindness, judgment, and righteousness in the
earth.'

Consider, again, how the Greeks regarded
the facts of history. They felt, first of all, the
intellectual curiosity to know what had really
happened. A fact was interesting because it
was true. The past was in itself worthy
of investigation, of tolerant and sympathetic
inquiry. We have here "ἱστορία" in its primary
sense as the search for truth. But no Greek
could treat history as a mere succession of facts,
a chance sequence of events. An explanation
of the facts must be sought, some unifying
principle discovered. Particulars must be
viewed in larger relations. The interpretative

force of mind must be brought to bear upon them, and their hidden meaning extracted. It is not the facts, but the meaning of the facts, that is of paramount interest; the facts must, if possible, be made into truths. And it is remarkable with what intellectual insight the great historians of Greece do actually apprehend the wider significance of the special chapters in Greek history which they severally narrate.

The conflict of Greece and Persia was for Herodotus the culminating point of a great drama, a clash of forces rendered inevitable by events that had been long preparing in the kingdoms of the East. Thucydides saw in the Peloponnesian war and in the tragedy of the Athenian downfall, an inner crisis affecting national character. Polybius recognised that with the empire of Rome new historical perspectives were opened up, and countries hitherto disconnected drawn into the current of universal history. Each of these writers was in his own way a philosophic historian. We have already seen in what sense this is true of

Herodotus.[1]   To penetrate the mind of Thucydides is a less easy task.   In his austere reserve
he is far removed from the ingenuous charm
and candour of Herodotus.   He is not ready
to come forward and reason with us.   He has
no intimate confidences to bestow.   He offers
few reflections containing a moral judgment.
While the moral impression is clear and sharp,
the award of praise or blame is left to the
reader.   Thucydides is concerned with understanding rather than with judging ; his aim is
to throw light on the laws of human action
and the permanent principles of conduct ;
to enable the statesman to direct the present
and in some measure to forecast the future.
He is under no illusions.   Psychological facts
are often unlovely enough : he records them
coldly : but to regard him as cynically indifferent is to misread the severe impartiality of
his art.   He felt the sombre fascination of the
Peloponnesian war, its terror and grandeur.
Great passions were there aroused, destructive
energies let loose, issuing in deeds both of

[1] Supr. p. 32.

savagery and heroism. The outward events were for the historian a material which must be rendered in terms of mind. His philosophic impulse shows itself in tracing causes ; not final causes, as with Herodotus ; but the secondary causes which are revealed on the stage of human life and in the heart of the actors. He does not profess to read the purposes of a supernatural power. Neither destiny nor chance is for him the governing force of the world. Events have their roots in character, of which they are the outcome ; it is here that we must seek their inner meaning. They are not mere startling or dramatic incidents, but phenomena whose reason lies deep in the moral disposition of nations and individuals, and the law of whose succession can be discovered. The great agent in shaping outward circumstances is the human will. The historian, therefore, who would interpret the world of facts must analyse the various forms in which mind manifests itself, must study its laws and reach the vital forces which are at work below the surface. History is a scroll written by human intelligence in the large and

I

legible letters of the past.   Thus, Thucydides
is a philosophic historian, but he expounds no
theory : he remains a historian, he is not a
philosopher—a historian, however, of imaginative insight who brings out both the poetry and
the philosophy latent in the facts.

Polybius, writing between two and three
centuries later, derives his guiding principles
direct from Thucydides.   He narrates the
struggle between Rome and Carthage for the
supremacy of the world ; and his design is to
exhibit the organic unity of history, the idea of a
universal history corresponding, as he conceived
it, to the fact of universal empire.   It is this
' clear œcumenical view,' says Freeman, ' which
makes him the teacher of all time.'   Unfortunately his style is a serious deterrent to the reader.
We long for the ease, the finished grace, the flowing simplicity of Herodotus ; or again, for the
terse and rapid phrase of Thucydides, the energy,
the precision of each single word, the sentence
packed with thought.   Polybius has lost the
Greek artistic feeling for writing, the delicate
sense of proportion, the faculty of reserve.   The

freshness and distinction of the Attic idiom are
gone.   He writes with an insipid and colourless
monotony.   In arranging his materials he is
equally inartistic.   He is always anticipating
objections and digressing ; he wearies you with
dilating on the excellence of his own method; he
even assures you that the size and price of his
book ought not to keep people from buying it.
Yet admirable as is the substance of his writing,
he pays the penalty attaching to neglect of
form——he is read by the few.   His interest,
however, for us here is that, while he intends
his history to be a practical treatise, containing
useful lessons for men of affairs, he is true to
the philosophic tradition he has inherited from
Thucydides, in his persistent effort to exhibit
the relations of cause and effect through the
texture of the narrative.   In particular, he is at
pains to search out the true cause of an event,
as distinguished from the occasion of its happen-
ing ; and such causes he follows back to their
source in character.   National life, like individual life, has for him an ethical basis ; it is in
character, and the institutions that grow out of

character, that the true movement of a people's
history is revealed.

The idea that the true causes of events
lie deep in character was appropriated as a
theory of history by Polybius : Demosthenes
had long ago received it from Thucydides as
an inspiring motive of civic eloquence.[1] The
Athenians, when defeated by Philip, were wont
to lay the blame on their politicians or their
generals, on adverse winds, on unkindly fortune.
Demosthenes carries the failure back to themselves—to their own indolence and improvi-
dence. He will not be put off with superficial
explanations. Character with him is all in all.
Every *Philippic* oration is instinct with the
thought. 'Is Philip dead ? No, he is only
ill. Dead or ill, what difference to you ? If
anything befals him, you will instantly create
another Philip for yourselves.'[2] Or again :
'Always letting slip the present and imagining
that the future will take care of itself, it is we
that have made Philip great and exalted him

[1] See S. H. Butcher, *Demosthenes* (Macmillan and Co.),
p. 144.   [2] *Phil.* i. 11.

to a height of power above that of any previous king of Macedon.'[1]   Men who can hope to succeed must have a mind that can anticipate and control outward circumstances : but in politics, as in war, the Athenians 'wait upon events'; they begin to think when the time has come for action; they strike after the blow has fallen.[2]

The use of opportunity, the strong man's ability to seize the present and to shape the future, is a favourite topic of Demosthenes. Its full significance may best be read in connexion with the Greek idea of *Kairos* (καιρός) in literature and art.   No other nation has distinguished so subtly the different forms under which time can be logically conceived. *Chronos* (χρόνος) is time viewed in its extension, as a succession of moments, the external framework of action.   Under this aspect of simple duration Time achieves, it is true, a silent work of its own.   Man cannot ignore its revealing power.   He looks on and almost unconsciously learns his lesson.   The arts, the sciences, come

[1] *Olynth*. i. 9.   [2] *Phil*. i. 39-41.

into being under its gradual influence. 'Time as it ages teaches all things'[1]; 'Time alone is the proof of real truth,'[2] the 'touch-stone of every deed,'[3] the one 'wisest thing.'[4] The phrases in which Aristotle describes Time as agent or joint-agent in the work of progressive discovery,[5] bear an impressive resemblance to the thought and language of Bacon. *Chronos*, however, remained on the whole too abstract, too indeterminate to admit easily of personal embodiment in literature or art. It was otherwise with *Kairos*—a word which has, I believe, no single or precise equivalent in any

[1] Aesch. *P. V.* 981 :

    ἀλλ' ἐκδιδάσκει πάνθ' ὁ γηράσκων χρόνος.

[2] Pind. *Ol.* xi. 59-61 :

    ὅ τ' ἐξελέγχων μόνος
    ἀλάθειαν ἐτήτυμον
    Χρόνος.

[3] Simon. of Cos Fr. 175 :

    οὐκ ἔστιν μείζων βάσανος χρόνου οὐδενὸς ἔργου.

[4] A saying of Thales (quoted Plut. *Conv. vii Sap.* 9) in answer to the question τί σοφώτατον ;—Χρόνος · τὰ μὲν γὰρ εὕρηκεν οὗτος ἤδη, τὰ δὲ εὑρήσει. Cp. Bacon *Aphor.* xxxii. 'Sapientissima autem res tempus (ut ab antiquis dictum est) et novorum casuum quotidie auctor et inventor.'

[5] Arist. *Nic. Eth.* i. 7. 17 δόξειε δ' ἂν . . . ὁ χρόνος τῶν τοιούτων εὑρετὴς ἢ συνεργὸς ἀγαθὸς εἶναι.

other language. *Kairos* is that immediate
present which is what we make it; Time
charged with opportunity; our own possession,
to be seized and vitalised by human energy;
momentous, effectual, decisive; Time the inert
transformed into purposeful activity. Not
only did the poet Ion compose a hymn to
Kairos in which he is called the youngest child
of Zeus—opportunity being truly thought of
as the latest and god-given gift—but in art the
rendering of *Kairos* is various and interesting.
Sometimes he is a youth pressing forward with
wings on his feet and back, holding a pair of
scales, which he inclines with a slight touch of
the right hand to one side. His hair is long
in front and bald behind; he must be grasped,
if at all, by the fore-lock. In one relief, where
Kairos occupies the centre, *Regret* (Μετάνοια)
is represented as a shrinking and dejected
form who stands beside an old man, symbol-
ising the sadness felt over the lost moment
that cannot be recalled. In the palæstra—
and here he is most at home—*Kairos* appears
in the guise of a Hermes, an athlete god. It

is *Kairos* who seizes the lucky moment in the wrestling bout ; *Kairos* who with his chariot-wheels closely grazes the goal ; *Kairos* to whom men offered sacrifice as they entered the stadium. *Kairos* is the god of the man with a mind swift but sure in decision, and with a body trained to be the mind's obedient servant. The sense of the opportune that is here suggested is as unlike as possible to what is commonly known as 'opportunism' ; it is 'the triumphant flash of daring and right judgment' ; it goes with high originality and initiative, and reaches even to the point of genius.

Thucydides and Demosthenes had the same ideal of statesmanship. Great men are those in whom the power of the spirit dominates matter. Their strong intelligence, free from illusion, their calm and clear reflection does not issue in any hesitating purpose ; it leads direct to action. They know how to seize occasion ; they are masters of things outward ; they go boldly forth to meet the incalculable thing we call fortune ; they thrust obstacles aside or fall, if needs must be, in the attempt.   It is a view akin to that of tragedy, where external actions and events are but the setting in which character is displayed ; where, in a much more complete and deeper sense, man can prove himself to be not the creature, but the lord of circumstances, which he moulds in the strength of his spiritual energy.   Just as in the region of creative art the imagination impresses its own form on the lifeless elements, remaking them with its touch ; so too the Greek philosopher, historian, orator, each proclaims in divers ways the supremacy of spiritual over material forces ; each brings some new outlying territory under the domain of reason.

We have followed the working of the Greek intellect as revealed not in a passive reception of ideas, but in the energetic action it brings to bear on all that comes within its range : it correlates, interprets, unifies the facts of experience ; translates outward things into terms of spirit, transmuting all dead material.   The views of Greek thinkers on Education are in accord with this attitude of mind.   With all

their restless curiosity, their insatiable love of
knowledge, they had no respect for mere
erudition. 'Wealth of thought, not wealth
of learning' was the thing they coveted :—
πολυνοΐην, οὐ πολυμαθίην ἀσκεῖν χρή, is the
striking saying of Democritus.[1] Heraclitus,
Plato, Aristotle, all speak in similar depreciatory
terms of mere ' polymaths '—men of multifarious
learning, untouched by the quickening force of
reason. Extensive reading, the acquisition of
facts, the storing of them in the memory—all
this is possible without any discipline or
enlargement of mind. In order that learning
may become wisdom two conditions must be
satisfied. First, the facts must be assimilated
and interpreted ; the formative power of thought
must work upon the material of knowledge.
And, secondly, learning must be humanised.
True learning is bound up with human fellowship. It is a partnership in which there is
give and take, a joint search and joint discovery.
To the Greeks the subject taught seemed of

[1] Democr. ap. Stob. iii. 4. 81.   Cp. *Ib.* πολλοὶ πολυμαθέες
νόον οὐκ ἔχουσι.

less importance than the man who taught it. The teacher's office was to show the right method of learning. He himself is a learner, who in and through learning becomes a teacher. Just as Greek poetry, more than that of any other nation, is the expression of the people's collective, life, so Greek learning draws its inspiration not so much from solitary study as from noble companionship and ideal human intercourse. Education, as the Greeks conceived it, was based on broad and deep sympathy—sympathy of intellect and character, and sympathy of aim. The Pythagorean motto κοινὰ τὰ τῶν φίλων, 'Friends have all things in common,' might have been written over every Greek class-room. The love of truth, the spirit of joint investigation, the 'following of the argument whithersoever it leads'—this was the bond of union, the prized possession of the brotherhood of learning.

There is one salient difference between education as understood by the Greeks and the popular idea of education in our own day. To the Greeks education was primarily a train-

ing of faculty that should fit men for the
exercise of thought and the duties of citizenship.   The modern world looks rather to the
acquisition of some skill or knowledge that is
needed for a career; it thinks more of the
product than of the process.   Acquaintance
with facts counts more with the modern;
mental completeness and grasp are primary
with the Greek.   But that mental completeness
was not to be won through intellectual discipline alone; it meant also a discipline and
moulding of character, a training in public
spirit, a suppression of the individual, a devotion
to civic ends.   The Greek *Paideia* (παιδεία) in
its full sense involves the union of intellectual
and moral qualities.   It is on the one hand
mental illumination, an enlarged outlook on
life; but it also implies a refinement and
delicacy of feeling, a deepening of the sympathetic emotions, a scorn of what is self-seeking,
ignoble, dishonourable—a scorn bred of loving
familiarity with poets and philosophers, with
all that is fortifying in thought or elevating in
imagination.   Our nearest equivalent for this

generous and many-sided training is Culture ;
but unfortunately the word has acquired a
tinge of meaning that is alien to the Greek
Paideia. Culture to many minds suggests
a kind of polish, a superficial refinement.
Besides, it has about it an air of exclusiveness ;
it is thought of as the privilege of a favoured
few.   The man of learning in modern times is
too apt to remain in seclusion ; he seems to be
shut up within a charmed circle, in possession
of a secret hidden from the many ; and the
impression not unfrequently left on outsiders
by the life of learned isolation is conveyed in
the remark of a French writer, that ' every man
of learning is more or less of a corpse.'   Now
Greek culture in its ideal form is a connecting
link between learning and citizenship ; it is a
meeting-point of virtue and knowledge, an outcome of character, an attitude of the whole
mind towards life.   The intellectual *élite* are
not estranged from the life of the community.
Learning is thus humanised ; instead of a dead
weight of erudition it becomes a living force, a
civilising and liberating power.   We have here

the spirit of a University in its true conception.
One chief function of academic training should
be to foster this broad view of learning ; and,
in so doing, incidentally to disprove the saying :
'Gentlemen are untaught by the World what
they have been taught by the College.'[1]

A tincture of Greek is, fortunately, no
longer regarded as a hall-mark of good breed-
ing, or a sign that one has acquired at College
a few gentlemanly vices.   And the popular
mind has, therefore, jumped to the conclusion
that Greek has ceased to have any value except to furnish barbarous compounds for the
advertisement of a new umbrella or of a quack-
medicine.   The call to burn our unlawful books
of Greek is heard from many sides.   But those
who care for the deeper principles of education
will never cease to go back to what the Greeks
have said or hinted on this theme.   All great
teachers have been Greek in spirit.   Education, in the Greek view, is the antithesis of any
mere specialism, and that in two senses.   It
emancipates us from the narrowing influence

[1] Berkeley, *Minute Phil.* Dial. v. 24.

of a trade or a purely professional calling, and
lifts us into the higher air of liberal studies.
But also, even within the domain of learning,
we are reminded that expert knowledge may
itself become a contraction of the intellect ;
and that the thoroughness of the craftsman,
the minute work of the investigator, must not
lead the teacher to miss the larger relations of
his subject, and lose sight of the whole.   Nor
can we forget that the man himself is behind
what he says or writes.   Plato observes that
for the higher forms of literary composition the
name of writer or author is an inadequate
description : the title is well enough for one
who has nothing in him greater than the
phrases he puts on paper (τὸν μὴ ἔχοντα
τιμιώτερα ὧν συνέθηκεν ἢ ἔγραψεν).[1]   And a
similar remark may be made about the teacher.
As Life is something beyond Literature, so
Personality is something beyond Learning.
The teacher who leaves an impress on other
minds is greater than his own knowledge,
greater than the information he conveys.   This

[1] Plat. *Phaedr.* 278 D–E.

is true of all teachers who have in any degree succeeded in making their appeal to that mighty and half-utilised force—the idealistic impulses of youth ; and from this point of view Teaching—as I believe some one has said —while it is the vilest of trades becomes the noblest of professions.

IV

ART AND INSPIRATION IN GREEK
POETRY

GREEK literature is the one entirely original
literature of Europe. With no models before
their eyes to provoke imitation or rivalry, the
Greeks created almost every form of literary
art—the epic, the lyric, the elegy, the drama,
the dialogue, the idyll, the romantic novel,
history, and oratory ; and the permanence of
the types so created shows that they rest on
no arbitrary rules or on the mannerisms of a
people, but answer to certain artistic laws of
the human mind. We who see for the most
part only the perfected forms, are apt to
forget what varied and repeated experiments,
what frequent failures, must have gone to the
making of each of these types. In the *Poetics*

Aristotle notes the gradual and tentative process by which special metres proved themselves adapted to the several kinds of poetry—
the iambic to tragedy, the hexameter to epic
song.   They are instances, as we should say,
of the survival of the fittest: ἀπὸ τῆς πείρας
ἥρμοκεν [1]—that is Aristotle's phrase.   The
process here indicated was a familiar idea to
the Greeks.   Popular observation summed it
up in the simple proverbial form, πεῖρα ἄριστον,
' nothing like experiment.'   It is the sentiment
which Herodotus puts into the mouth of
Mardonius : ' Nothing comes of its own accord
to men, but all things by experiment.' [2]   On
the same principle tragedy itself, as Aristotle
remarks, ' having passed through many changes
found its natural form, and there it stopped.' [3]
Man's selective instinct, working tentatively,

---

[1] Arist. *Poet.* xxiv. 5 τὸ δὲ μέτρον τὸ ἡρωικὸν ἀπὸ τῆς πείρας
ἥρμοκεν.   Cp. iv. 9 ἐν οἷς καὶ τὸ ἁρμόττον [ἰαμβεῖον] ἦλθε
μέτρον.

[2] Herod. vii. 9 αὐτόματον γὰρ οὐδέν, ἀλλ' ἀπὸ πείρης πάντα
ἀνθρώποισι φιλέει γενέσθαι.

[3] Arist. *Poet.* iv. 12 πολλὰς μεταβολὰς μεταβαλοῦσα ἡ
τραγῳδία ἐπαύσατο, ἐπεὶ ἔσχε τὴν αὐτῆς φύσιν.

brought the process of development to its proper term.

When once any particular type was created, it assumed its sharp Hellenic outline. No blurred image, no confusion of kinds was permissible. Any deviation from the type fell within well-defined limits. Each branch of literature obeyed a stringent code of its own. Its governing traditions answered to an artistic sense that art to be progressive must also be conservative. It must maintain a spirit of reverent regard for the past. Old material must be used up : new ideas, whether of native origin or due to the absorption of foreign influences, must be slowly assimilated. If in political history we meet with revolutionary violence, in literary as in artistic development there is growth and orderly advance. The whole effort of Greek literature is to evolve itself in unbroken sequence, without the rude snapping of any links which bind the present to the past, with no premature rejection of existing elements.

Yet the persistent force of tradition did not

check the free play of individual genius. With
the observance of a strict artistic code and the
accepted conventions of a school, the literary
art was not hardened into mere formalism. The
more rigorous the rules, the greater the triumph
of genius in obeying them without effort. In
tragedy the poets at first ranged at will over the
whole field of legendary story.[1] The domain
of the drama was by degrees restricted.
But the narrower limits within which freedom
was henceforth possible stimulated rather than
checked dramatic originality. The inventive
faculty found ample scope in re-interpreting
the known cycle of legends with subtle and
significant divergence in detail. 'Great and
precious origination,' says George Eliot, 'can
only exist on condition of a wide massive
uniformity. When a multitude of men have
learned to use the same language in speech and
writing, then and then only can the greatest
matters of language arise. For in what does
their mastery consist? They use words which
are already a familiar medium of understand-

[1] Arist. *Poet.* xiii. 15.

ing and sympathy in such a way as greatly
to enlarge the understanding and sympathy.'
This that is said in the first instance of style, is
in its measure also true of the handling of the
subject-matter.   The creative act of genius does
not consist in bringing something out of nothing,
but in taking possession of material that exists,
in appropriating it, interpreting it anew.   The
original force of the Greek poet stamps all rude
material with the mark of the race—'made in
Greece.'

The treatment of the Chorus in the drama is
perhaps the most signal instance of the power
of the poet to turn to account a consecrated
tradition.   Here was an undramatic element,
that was yet an indispensable part of every
play—a religious survival from an early stage
of the undeveloped art.   The chorus was a
collective personage, with a character shifting
and ill-defined, an awkward presence on the
stage and often out of keeping with the poetic
illusion.   In Aeschylus it is generally what Aristotle in the *Poetics* (ch. xviii. 7) says the chorus
ought to be—'one of the actors'; in Sophocles

more often it fulfils the function assigned to it
in Aristotle's *Problems* (xix. 48) ; it is a κηδευτὴς
ἄπρακτος, one who does not act but who is in
intimate or friendly relation with some of the
actors ; an interested spectator or a kindly
sympathiser.[1] Who would have thought that
an element apparently so inartistic could have
been anything but a mere encumbrance, a
clog on the action—as indeed it became in
Euripides—a structural flaw in the composition?

Yet this ambiguous personage plays a great
part. It forms a connecting link between
the actors and the audience. Whatever its
sympathies may have been in the piece, it
generally manages in the end to place itself in
the attitude of an impartial witness. In comedy
it pronounces the verdict on the ἀγών—that
pitched battle between the combatants—which
is distinctive of this branch of the drama. In
tragedy it seldom fails to utter the last word.
At certain moments of the play it provides a
contemplative pause, an interlude for moralising

---

[1] εὔνοιαν γὰρ μόνον παρέχεται οἷς πάρεστιν.

reflection.   In Aeschylus, it becomes the vehicle
of the poet's profoundest theological thought ;
in Sophocles, more frequently it interprets the
course of the action and sums up the emotions
awakened in the spectator's mind.   In either
case, the choral odes, apart altogether from their
intrinsic beauty as forms of lyrical and musical
utterance, gather up for us the lessons of life   •
and clarify our human experience.   Those great
and eternal commonplaces in which Greek
poetry delights, with their measured cadence,
their serene and condensed wisdom, have a
strange power of solemnising and subduing the
emotions.   They come home to us in all the
fulness of their original meaning, as familiar
truths fraught with new significance.   The
tension of overwrought feeling is relaxed when
the fret and stir of the moment, and the accidents
of the individual existence, are placed in the
larger perspective of some universal law.   In
almost every branch of literature we have
similar achievements.   The great writers, by
the very force of their individuality, accept
with ease much that is conventional, while they

reject what is merely artificial.[1] The more closely we examine the masterpieces of Greek literature, the greater appears to be the place occupied by artistic tradition and convention. Thus Greece presents a phenomenon unique in literary history—namely, the creation of fixed types, governed by a rigid code of rules, yet working in harmony with the spontaneous play of native faculty.

This continuity of movement in art and literature involved some self-suppression on the part of the individual. While the collective

[1] The history of sculpture affords many analogous examples. See the remarks on the Metopes and Frieze of the Parthenon in a recent volume, *Greek Sculpture*, by E. von Mach, Boston (Ginn and Co.), 1903, p. 216 ff.; compare also pp. 156-160. Similarly in vase-painting, the restrictions of space and the conditions of decorative art force the artist to recognise that the human body is not a human body only, but also a thing that is capable of being rendered as a beautiful pattern. The figures, therefore, are not thrown vaguely into a given space, but are closely tied up and related to the parts they do not fill. And the notable result is that these figures, by mutual adaptations and concessions, gain a heightened beauty through forming part of a decorative design. The feet of the dancing Maenads on Hieron's cup is a case in point. It is, of course, only the great masters who can so employ the limitations imposed. Lesser artists cramp their figures in obedience to physical necessity.

personality of the race is indelibly stamped on
the products of the Greek mind—on their art
and literature, even on their science—the
personality of the individual, though seldom to
be mistaken in the realm, at least, of imaginative
creation, does not appear in an obtrusive form.
The plastic clearness of outline which is
characteristic of the classical Greek manner is
mainly due to two causes :—on the one hand,
to the omission of accidental detail, on the other
to the absence of a disturbing atmosphere. In
the romantic handling of a theme the image is
apt to be seen through a sensitive and vibrat-
ing medium, through a coloured light, in the
' halo' of romance ; and the ' halo,' the atmosphere, is often caused in part by the excited
personality of the writer. He catches fire from
his own creation, he projects his personal trouble
into his art, and the contagion spreads to the
reader. The great classical writer remains
more detached ; he holds the image, so to speak,
at arm's length. The spectacle he presents
impresses us by its own moving quality ; there
is no personal or turbid atmosphere ; no per-

plexed light is interposed between our eye and
the object. We are still within the domain of
the universal reason.

Yet according to the popular view poetry
was a thing inspired—*ἔνθεον ἡ ποίησις* : [1] it
was a form of frenzy, a divine possession.
Poetic inspiration was regarded as supernatural
in its origin, the poet being but the channel
through which the god finds utterance ; he acts
under a stimulus from without, which robs him
of his reason. This theory of direct revelation
is explicitly stated in prose for the first time
by Democritus of Abdera ; [2] it is applied by
him to Homer ; it remains current to the latest
period of Greek literature. The idea of the
frenzied poet strikes us as having a strangely
un-Greek air. It seems to accord better with

---

[1] Arist. *Rhet.* iii. 7. 1408 b 19.

[2] Dio Chrys. *Or.* liii. ad init. ὁ μὲν Δημόκριτος περὶ Ὁμήρου
φησὶν οὕτως· "Ὅμηρος φύσεως λαχὼν θεαζούσης ἐπέων κόσμον
ἐτεκτήνατο παντοίων." Clem. *Strom.* vi. 168 p. 827 P καὶ ὁ
Δημόκριτος ὁμοίως (*i.e.* like Plato in the *Ion*) "ποιητὴς δὲ ἄσσα
μὲν ἂν γράφῃ μετ' ἐνθουσιασμοῦ καὶ ἱεροῦ πνεύματος, καλὰ
κάρτα ἐστίν." Cic. *de divin.* I. 38, 80 'negat enim sine furore
Democritus quemquam poëtam magnum esse posse, quod idem
dicit Plato.'

Oriental notions, or with modern speculations about the subliminal self as the region out of which emerge both poetry and insanity. ⌈The Greek poets themselves seem to have thought of their own aptitude more as the result of trained skill than of abnormal inspiration. It is remarkable how the word σοφία, 'wisdom,' 'skill,' is selected by them to denote the poetic gift where we should be disposed to speak of genius.[1]⌉ We are not greatly surprised when a poet like Bacchylides, conscious perhaps of no high originality, speaks of poetry as so much traditional lore : 'Poet from poet learns his art both now and of old.'[2]

But the case of Pindar is more striking. No poet, it is true, dwells with such conviction on inborn power of genius as surpassing all the efforts of art. 'Nature's gift is always supreme : where the god is not, silence is ever the better part of wisdom.'[3] ⌈'He is the

---

[1] *Some Aspects of the Greek Genius*, p. 17.

[2] Bacchyl. Fr. 14 [13] ἕτερος ἐξ ἑτέρου σοφὸς τό τε πάλαι τό τε νῦν.

[3] Pind. *Ol.* ix. 100 ff. τὸ δὲ φυᾷ κράτιστον ἅπαν | . . . ἄνευ δὲ θεοῦ σεσιγαμένον | οὐ σκαιότερον χρῆμ' ἕκαστον.

skilled poet to whom nature has taught much.'[1]
Proudly he avows his own originality, his
daring novelty of treatment: 'To many have
I shown the ways of song.'[2] Yet he also
exalts to the utmost the influence of art. His
poetry is a subtle science, which obeys laws of
its own, fixed rules or ordinances,[3] transmitted
by the masters of the craft. And modern
research has brought into marked prominence
the long development of the lyrical art, and
the fashioning of a special vocabulary ; it has
analysed the elaborate structure of a Pindaric
ode, and shown not only the trained skill
implied in the poetic handling of the myths,
but the science needed to combine the complex
resources of metre and music, and adapt them
to the intricate choral dance. Truly, as Pindar
says, 'steep are the heights of the poetic art';[4]
and although they cannot be scaled without the
inborn gift, yet nowhere more surely than in

---

[1] *Ol.* ii. 86 σοφὸς ὁ πολλὰ εἰδὼς φυᾷ : *i.e.* the true σοφία is φύσις.

[2] *Pyth.* iv. 247 πολλοῖσι δ' ἥγημαι σοφίας ἑτέροις.

[3] Cp. *Ol.* vii. 88 ὕμνου τεθμὸς 'Ολυμπιονίκος.

[4] *Ol.* ix. 115 σοφίαι μὲν αἰπειναί.

Greek lyric song did nature need the assistance
of art.[1]

The popular theory of poetry as a divine
possession perhaps owed its origin to the fact
that direct revelation, in its most familiar form
of mantic or oracular utterances, was conveyed
in metrical language. The mystery of the poetic
gift could best be accounted for by suppos-
ing that the poet was the inspired interpreter
of the Muse as the Pythian priestess was of
the Delphic deity. Pindar himself appropriates
the mythological phrases : ' Utter thy oracles,
O Muse, and I will be thy mouthpiece.'[2] It
was but a coarse form of the inspiration theory
which credited Aeschylus with composing his
tragedies in a state of intoxication.[3] In connexion with this bit of literary gossip Athenaeus
records the saying attributed to Sophocles :
' You, Aeschylus, do the right thing, but
without knowing why.'[4] It is just this ' οὐκ

---

[1] On Pindar as an artist cp. R. C. Jebb, *Growth and
Influence of Classical Poetry*, p. 160 ff.

[2] Pind. Fr. 127 [118] μαντεύεο Μοῖσα, προφατεύσω δ' ἐγώ.

[3] Athen. i. 39 p. 22 A and x. 33 p. 428 F.

[4] εἰ καὶ τὰ δέοντα ποιεῖς ἀλλ' οὐκ εἰδώς γε.

εἰδώς ' — the ' not knowing ' — that Plato accentuates in various passages, in which, adopting the current theory of inspiration, he speaks in severe disparagement of poetry. ' The poet,' he says,[1] ' when he sits down on the tripod of the Muses is not in his right mind. Like a fountain he allows the stream of thought to flow freely, and, his art being imitative, he is often compelled to represent men under opposite circumstances, and thus to say two different things ; neither could he tell whether there is any truth in either of them or in one more than in the other.' So in the *Apology*,[2] when Socrates goes to the poets and asks them the meaning of their own works, he finds them the most incompetent of all critics ; they can give no rational account of what they have written. ' They showed me in an instant that not by wisdom do men write poetry but by a sort of genius and inspiration ; they are like diviners and soothsayers who say many fine things, but do not understand the meaning

---

[1] Plat. *Laws* iv. p. 719 C.

[2] *Apol.* p. 22 A.

of them.' The poet, then, even when he speaks inspired truth[1] has no clear knowledge of the grounds of his beliefs ; he may also speak inspired falsehood. At the best he attains to right opinion, which, however, falls far short of knowledge.

The popular conception of the poet as an inspired madman, destitute of art, who can compose nothing so long as he is in his senses, leads Plato to a slighting appreciation of the poetic gift. But there is another side to the case, and this is developed by him in the *Phaedrus.* If the popular point of view merely brings the poet and the philosopher into sharp antithesis, the kinship between them is marked by another and nobler view of poetry as a revelation to sense of eternal ideas. Poet and philosopher, each alike is lifted out of himself. In this state of ' ecstasy,' when the soul is possessed by a passionate yearning after truth— a divine enthusiasm—it recalls the celestial world whence it came and catches a glimpse of the invisible or ideal beauty, of which the

[1] Cp. *Laws* iii. p. 682 A.

Eleusinian mysteries are a faint type. For the poet, as for the philosopher, the highest inspiration comes from the spiritual insight gained in this moment of rapture. The faculty of reminiscence which makes this beatific vision possible is for Plato the common principle of philosophy and poetry. The poet is possessed by an imaginative enthusiasm that is akin to the speculative enthusiasm of the philosopher.

Poetry is thus a stage in the upward progress of the soul; it is the servant of philosophy whose truths it dimly shadows forth. When fully perfected it is absorbed in a philosophy which through the manifold things of sense ascends to that highest sphere, where truth and beauty are one with virtue. In the *Phaedrus* and the *Symposium* Plato passes beyond the poetry of his own age and prefigures an art which has been realised, if at all, in Dante, in whom the speculations of philosophy, the visions of the poetic imagination, and a devotion to beauty and goodness, are blended together in one mystical passion. It is a world whose secrets can be unlocked only by those who like Plato and Dante are at once poets and prophets.

Plato's account of inspiration agrees in essentials with modern ideas. The metaphors in which he clothes his thought in the *Phaedrus* must not be allowed to disguise his true meaning. With him the inspiration of genius, whether poetic or philosophic, is not a direct revelation, operating as an influence from without, but one of the modes in which the soul puts forth certain divine powers inherent in her nature. These natural gifts, however, are quickened and kindled to higher activity. A new and rapturous energy springs up, inexplicable, unfamiliar, breaking in upon the monotony of common life. It achieves in a moment of insight what no effort of conscious thought can accomplish. The reason is not overpowered or the personality lost; but the man's self is raised above the normal level. It is no longer the self of the working-day existence; nor again is it an alien self; it is the true and highest self in which the lower one is merged. Poetic inspiration even on this lofty view of it, does not

L

dispense with conscious art; for the inspired moment often is but the sudden consummation of a long period of mental travail; and, moreover, even after the creative idea has flashed upon the mind, a conscious and shaping process is needed to give it complete embodiment. On the other hand, no one can be admitted into the higher ranks of poetry who is devoid of the inspired faculty. The more or less, however, in the matter of inspiration is a difference of degree which almost amounts to a difference of kind; and we commonly apply the term inspired only to those in whom the impression of spontaneous genius overmasters the impression of art.

Aristotle incidentally notes the difference between the two orders of poets: 'Poetry implies either a happy gift of nature or a strain of madness. In the one case a man can take the mould of any character, in the other he is lifted out of his proper self.'[1] The poet of the first

[1] Poet. xvii. 2 διὸ εὐφυοῦς ἡ ποιητική ἐστιν ἢ μανικοῦ· τούτων γὰρ οἱ μὲν εὔπλαστοι οἱ δὲ ἐκστατικοί εἰσιν. All MSS. but one have ἐξεταστικοί: but see S. H. Butcher, *Aristotle's Theory of Poetry and Fine Art*, third ed.

class is a man of flexible genius, with keen and
versatile intelligence, with a delicate power of
seeing resemblances.[1]   He is quick to receive the
impress of another personality, and to enter
dramatically into another's feelings.   Contrasted
with him is the poet who is touched with a fine
frenzy, possessed by an inspiration or enthusiasm
in virtue of which he is ' ecstatic ' ; he is readily
lifted out of himself and loses his own personality.
The εὐφυής here is marked off from the μανικός
by a more conscious critical faculty.   As
examples of the two contrasted types, one might
suggest Sophocles and Aeschylus, Bacchylides
and Pindar, Dryden and Marlowe, Beaumont and
Fletcher, M. Arnold and Blake.   The contrast
drawn by Aristotle is not expressed in such precise form in any previous writer, but the distinction was constantly present to the mind of
Plato ; it is developed and illustrated from many
points of view in the treatise *On the Sublime ;*
and indeed the idea is at the very basis of that

---

[1] Cp. *Poet.* xxii. 9 where command of metaphor (τὸ
μεταφορικὸν εἶναι) is εὐφυίας σημεῖον ; and the making of good
metaphors is τὸ τὸ ὅμοιον θεωρεῖν.

treatise.   The supreme excellence which the
author means to convey by the term ὕψος,
including not only sublimity in our sense, but
elevation of tone, a glow of imagination, a
grandeur of style, is the distinguishing mark of
the inspired writer.   He is raised into a higher
plane under the influence of noble emotion, and
produces on his hearers the effect not of persuasion but of 'transport' (ἔκστασις).[1]

The examples given are not only passages
in the poets, such as the prayer of Ajax in the
Iliad—ἐν δὲ φάει καὶ ὄλεσσον, 'Destroy us
but destroy us in the light,' or Sappho's great
ode φαίνεταί μοι κῆνος, but passages from Demosthenes, such as that containing the famous
oath in the speech *On the Crown*—μὰ τοὺς ἐν
Μαραθῶνι προκινδυνεύσαντας,—and the words
of the *Book of Genesis*, 'God said, Let there
be light: and there was light.'   Demosthenes
is cited as the master of such emotional
effects.   He may lack the fluent ease, the

---

[1] Longinus *De Subl.* c. i. 4 οὐ γὰρ εἰς πειθὼ τοὺς ἀκρωμένους
ἀλλ' εἰς ἔκστασιν ἄγει τὰ ὑπερφυᾶ.   Cp. iii. 5 ἐξεστηκότες πρὸς
οὐκ ἐξεστηκότας.

urbane and piquant charm of Hypereides, but his 'heaven-sent gifts' (θεόπεμπτα δωρήματα) leave him supreme above all rivals : 'he silences by his thunders and blinds by his lightnings the orators of every age.   One could sooner face with unflinching eyes a descending thunder-bolt than meet with steady gaze his bursts of passion in their swift succession.'[1]   Yet the final lesson to be gathered from the eloquence of Demosthenes is, as Longinus observes, that 'even in the revels of the imagination sobriety is required.'[2]   Here we have the true Hellenic note.   Speeches which are alive with the fire of passion have been laboriously prepared in the closet.   We never lose the impression of severe and disciplined strength.   In his highest outbursts of eloquence Demosthenes still owns the sway of reason.   'It is not possible with him, as with lesser orators, to map out a speech into parts and say here is an appeal to feeling ; here is pure reasoning ; for thought is

---

[1] *De Subl.* c. xxxiv. 4 ὡσπερεὶ καταβροντᾷ καὶ καταφέγγει τοὺς ἀπ' αἰῶνος ῥήτορας κ.τ.λ.   (Trans. H. L. Havell, Macmillan and Co.)

[2] *Ib.* c. xvi. 4 διδάσκων ὅτι κἂν βακχεύμασι νήφειν ἀναγκαῖον.

everywhere interpenetrated with feeling ; reason is itself passionate. What fuses all into unity is the force of an intense personality, which cannot convince the intellect without kindling the emotions.'[1]   The eloquence of Demosthenes is the eloquence of impassioned reason. The inspired orator is also the cool thinker and the consummate artist. A somewhat analogous fact meets us in the Sophoclean drama. In the very height of tragic suffering the actors are masters of themselves ; their vision is undisturbed, their judgment unclouded. They reason and reflect on what they have done. They place themselves in the attitude of criticism. Out of the depth of their anguish they seem to gain a heightened intellectual force, a more penetrating insight. When we are dealing with Greek literature we must beware not to separate too sharply thought and emotion, reason and inspiration.

Aristotle's distinction between the inspired poet and the finely gifted artist admits of rarer, or at least less striking, illustration from Greek

[1] S. H. Butcher, *Demosthenes*, p. 159.

than from modern literature. The imaginative creations of the modern world seldom unite in anything like equal proportions the twofold elements of art and inspiration. In Greek poetry these qualities are not often present in so disparate a form as to affect the general sense of harmony. Sometimes indeed the impression of inspired faculty, of original genius, in Greek poetry is a little obscured by the other impression of poetic art obeying the strict rules of a code. We take account of the conventional elements ; we note also the narrow range of poetic subject-matter ; and we are in danger of forgetting that genius often lies in creating much out of little ; that it wins its most signal triumphs from the very limitations within which it works. Again, the Greek perfection of form may itself lead moderns, who are imbued with the spirit of romantic literature, to underrate the original power which underlies such art. Genius, poetic inspiration, at once suggests—and truly suggests—to our minds a welling up of thought and feeling, an effortless and spontaneous energy, a sudden inrush of new emotion as the creative idea rises into consciousness. Aeschylus, we readily say, is an inspired poet, one who thinks in images, who sees intuitively where another reasons. We recognise in him the fervour of the prophet, whose words, instinct with passion, struggle to express thoughts which transcend the expressive capacity of speech. No wonder that the utterance is often rugged and inartistic. We are fain to believe that we see the workings of a hidden self, whose processes are higher than those of our normal intelligence, and whose swift insight discerns the way to its artistic result without employing the common logical links of thought. The saying ascribed to Sophocles, which has been already quoted, returns to our mind :—'You do the right thing, but you do it without knowing why.'

Yet this is a one-sided judgment. Aeschylus the inspired thinker is at the same time a great artist. And, similarly, Sophocles the conscious artist is none the less an inspired poet. If there is more of grandeur and mystery, a larger output of imaginative ideas in Aeschylus, there is more of a beauty which is itself an inspiration in Sophocles. It is a beauty of the distinctively Greek order, which results not from any sum of effects but from a harmony of effects, from a network of delicate relationships, from the subordination of the parts, and their convergence on a single end. It is a quiet unobtrusive beauty, in which the total impression is one of simplicity so perfect that it must needs be the product of consummate art. But a modern reader on first acquaintance with a play of Sophocles may well fail to realise that the constructive power which is capable of fashioning such a whole itself implies inspired insight, imaginative vision of the highest order. We are perhaps inclined to rate too low the genius which is displayed in the general structure of an artistic work ; we set it down merely as the hard-won result of labour, and we find inspiration only in isolated splendours, in the lightning flash of passion, in the revealing power of poetic imagery. The study of Greek literature leads us not indeed to undervalue these manifestations of genius, but to view all partial beauties in

their relation to the whole.   The supreme result
which Greek thought and imagination achieve
by their harmonious co-operation is the organic
union of the parts.   In the East the poetical
way of seeing things is that of direct intuition.
The East knows nothing of the dialectical
workings of the mind.   The service Greece
rendered lay in establishing the balance between
these faculties.   The emotional and intellectual
fields are no longer kept apart.   Reason and
intuition enter on a new alliance.   Greek artists
and poets have not indeed, like Mozart or
Wordsworth, left us any psychological account
of the processes of their own creative activity ;
and indeed the detailed working of these processes is generally hidden from the man of
genius himself.   In any case, it would be a
bold critic who would attempt to define in any
great imaginative composition the part played
by an instinctive or emotional element on the
one hand, and by logical thought on the other.

   But though we cannot say precisely how the
synthesis is effected in the mind of the creative
artist, we may safely apply a critical analysis to

the completed work of art. It matters not
whether some idea, to which the critic has been
guided only by a chain of reasoning, was flashed
instantaneously on the artistic vision. The interest of the analysis in the case of Greek art and
literature is this—that the parts are discovered
to be bound together by an inward, and
assuredly not an unconscious, logic. Especially
in architecture and the drama we can trace the
subordination of ideas. There is no room here
for caprice or happy accident. The elements
of thought and feeling, of reason and imagination have been fused together not in any
dim-lit region of sub-conscious thought. The
unified and artistic whole has been born in the
upper air ; it follows the laws of the universal
reason. 'There is not a single effect which
if not reasoned is not at least reasonable.' [1]
Moderns are prone to believe that the action
of poetic genius is purely instinctive or intuitive,
and that genius abdicates its rights and descends
to the lower level of talent when it begins to
reason. Greek literature decisively refutes such

[1] *Le Parthénon*, E. Boutmy, p. 201.

a notion.   It exhibits the critical faculty as
a great underlying element in creative power.
The analytic spirit of Aristotle's *Poetics* is not
to be explained solely by a certain prosaic
vein in the mind of the philosopher.   It is
distinctive of a race whose highest flights of
imagination are controlled by reasoned principles
of art, and whose creative work cannot be disjoined from the dialectic effort of thought.

The union of contrasted qualities which we
have been considering in the special field of
imaginative production is but one example of a
characteristic, which more eminently perhaps
than any other, constitutes the originality of
Greece.   We trace it in Greek life as well as in
Greek literature, in the impressive personalities
who stand out not only as actors in Greek
history, but also as writers and thinkers.   In
the history of Rome the man is often sunk in
the Roman ; his features are in low relief ; we
are led to forget the individual in the type.   In
Greece great personalities, with an ineffaceable
stamp of their own, are far more numerous—
men not only great in the things which they

accomplished, but interesting in themselves, in endowments of mind and force of character, in the union of many outwardly discordant gifts —idiosyncrasies, it may be, but the idiosyncrasies of genius. Illustrations might be drawn from all branches of Greek literature and from all periods ; I will confine myself to a rapid glance at that early period, the sixth to the fifth century B.C., before poetry was severed from philosophy or philosophy from science ; when thought and action were not yet divorced; when specialised knowledge and pursuits had not limited, and in limiting, also obscured the wonderful variety of powers residing in the gifted individual of the Hellenic race.[1]

We recall first Thales of Miletus, in the beginning of the sixth century B.C., the earliest of Greek philosophers, a man of science, a mathematician, one of the founders of the deductive Greek geometry, an astronomer who predicted the total eclipse of the sun which occurred in the war

[1] The philosophers, whose names are here selected for purposes of illustration, are, among others, brilliantly handled by Gomperz, *Greek Thinkers*, vol i. (Trans.).

between Lydia and Media on May 28, 585 B.C.
—a memorable prediction, the first of the kind
recorded in European history[1] — one whom
tradition remembered as the typical philosopher
who tumbled into a well while gazing at the
stars.[2]   But he was also a traveller, a shrewd
man of business, who turning to account his
meteorological researches is said to have made
the first 'corner' in oil;[3] a politician, moreover, of singular insight, who, if we may
believe Herodotus, advised his Ionian fellow-
countrymen to form a federal state with its
capital at Teos as a protection against
Persia.[4]

Or, again, take Xenophanes of Colophon
(flor. *circ.* 545 B.C.), the founder of the Eleatic
school of philosophy, who at the age of twenty-
five was driven from his Ionian home by the
Persian invasion, and for nearly threescore
years, by the testimony of his own verses,
'tossed his troubled thoughts up and down

---

[1] Herod. i. 74 ; Clem. *Strom.* i. 65 p. 354 P.

[2] Plat. *Theaet.* 174 A.

[3] Arist. *Pol.* i. 11. 1259 a 6 ; Diog. Laert. i. 26.

[4] Herod. i. 170.

Hellas' ;[1] a rhapsodist and a wandering philosopher, attended by a slave who carried his
cithara.   In the course of his travels he made
valuable scientific observations.   He was the
first who pointed to the fossil remains of plants
and animals as proofs of the great changes that
the earth must have undergone in the remote
past.   He broke sharply with the traditions
and beliefs of his people.   He is a satirist who
does not spare any of the institutions of Hellas—
the athletic games of Olympia any more than
the unimproving conversation of the dinner
table.   But it is as a religious reformer that
he utters his deepest convictions.   He passes
scathing criticism upon the beliefs of polytheism.   His passionate verses, introducing the
first note of discord between polytheism and
philosophy, echoed in the ears of the Greeks
throughout their history, and are again over-
heard in the final conflict between the de-

---

[1] Xenoph. Fr. 24 :

  ἤδη δ' ἑπτά τ' ἔασι καὶ ἑξήκοντ' ἐνιαυτοὶ ·
  βλησρίζοντες ἐμὴν φροντίδ' ἀν' Ἑλλάδα γῆν.

The word βλησρίζω is used in Hippocrates for tossing on a bed
of sickness.

fenders of expiring paganism and the Christian apologists.

Let us pass to another man even more remarkable, a poet-philosopher of brilliant genius, Empedocles of Agrigentum, of Dorian not Ionian race, some features of whose character are singularly un-Hellenic, though none but a pure Hellene could have written the noble hexameters of which some five hundred are extant. His poem *On Nature* was one of the books which inspired Lucretius, whose magnificent eulogy every one will remember.[1] As poet and physicist, with a wide outlook into the universal life of things, Empedocles traced a unity running through all natural and spiritual processes. He made original observations on physiology, ingenious experiments illustrating some laws of physics ; he threw out hints of the doctrine now known as natural selection, and anticipated some great discoveries of modern chemistry.[2] He was a practical physician and sanitary engineer as well as a

[1] Lucret. i. 716 ff.
[2] Gomperz, i. 230 (Trans.).

biologist, and by draining the marshes rid the city of Selinus of a pestilence. No ancient philosopher of whom we read took such a leading part in public life; he was the eloquent champion of the democracy and was offered and refused the kingship.[1] Aristotle tells us that he was also the founder of the art of rhetoric; and Gorgias of Leontini was said to be among his pupils.[2]

But there was also another side to him. He was a seer, a mystic, a healer of the maladies of the soul as well as of the body, the author of purificatory chants of which fragments survive. In outward demeanour he resembled the wonder-worker from the East rather than the sober Hellene. Clad in purple robe, with a Delphic wreath on his head and a golden circlet about his brows, his long hair flung loose, with grave set features he was borne in pomp through Sicily, the children flocking to his car, and the towns-people greeting him in his progress.[3] He is

---

[1] Diog. Laert. viii. 63.
[2] Arist. ap. Diog. Laert. viii. 57.
[3] Diog. Laert. viii. 73.

M

by his own description a spirit in exile,[1] one
of those heavenly beings, who for crime done
in another life are doomed 'to wander for
thrice ten thousand years away from the
Blessed,' tossed from sea to sky, from earth to
sea,

> and who returns
> Back to this meadow of calamity,
> This uncongenial place, this human life,—[2]

the 'unlovely land,' 'the unfamiliar region.'
Nor can the disinherited spirit regain his birthright except by long and rigorous discipline
and suppression of the senses. But I cannot
linger over this strange, this unique figure in
Greek speculation, in whom mysticism and
science, intuition and logic, religious exaltation
and practical capacity, the humility of a sin-
laden spirit and the boundless pretensions of a
charlatan were united to form so baffling a
compound. To this day in Girgenti, that
memorable city, where rows of ruined temples
guard the southern slopes of the acropolis,
stretching towards the sea, Empedocles is a

---

[1] Καθαρμοί, line 12, φυγὰς θεόθεν καὶ ἀλήτης.
[2] Matthew Arnold, *Empedocles on Aetna.*

name of power ; he is the idol of his fellow-countrymen ; legend and history still cluster round him.

I will but remind you of one other name—the founder of the famous Pythagorean brotherhood, which formed a close intellectual and spiritual partnership whose aim was the ennobling of the whole life, public and private, of its members.   Pythagoras himself was a mystical theologian and at the same time an original mathematician ; an astronomer who showed that the earth is spherical ; a musician who made a brilliant discovery in the theory of sound ;[1] a man of genius who, like Socrates, committed nothing to writing—from mistrust, it would seem, of the written word ; but whose personal influence so lived in the school as to leave an abiding mark on speculative thought long after the brotherhood itself had been dissolved by the violence of political faction.

What is it that constitutes the striking and original quality of such characters — of the physicist who is also a merchant ; the religious

[1] Gomperz, i. 102 (Trans.).

reformer, who is at once minstrel, poet, and
man of science ; the practical engineer who
has the soul of a mystic ; the mathematician
who is the head of a semi-religious order?
The secret lies in the harmonious blending of
opposites.   Such contrasts are not indeed confined to Greece ; but elsewhere they are rare
phenomena : in Greece these, or other not
widely dissimilar combinations, are part of the
normal psychology of those original minds
that have left their stamp upon the intellectual
life of Europe.   We see in them the con-
junction of a rich, an inexhaustible imagination
with a keen critical faculty, a restless, wondering, questioning spirit, fearless of consequences,
bringing all things to the test of reason.   We
see also a generalising power, constructive and
masterly, but apt to be over-hasty, balanced
however and corrected by a faculty of subtle
analysis and a delicate eye for differences in
detail.   Again, we observe the love of pointed
antithesis, visible in the very structure of the
sentence and form of the thought, in philo-
sophical conceptions (*e.g.* unity and plurality,

finite and infinite, Being and not Being, rest
and motion, etc.), in the balanced and contrasted groups of character within the drama.

Yet, quick as were the Greeks to discern antagonisms in the world of nature or
of man, it was also the conscious effort of
Greek philosophy to reconcile the discordant
principles, to build the bridge by which
thought might travel across the gulf, and so
by a finely graduated series of transitions
to restore the broken unity. Heraclitus of
Ephesus (born probably about 540 B.C.), anticipating a fruitful idea of modern philosophy,
laid down the law of the harmony of contraries, of identity in difference. Contraries
do not exclude, but rather presuppose one
another ; nay, each passes imperceptibly into
the other. 'The dissonant is in harmony with
itself.'[1] 'The invisible harmony'—which lies
behind the contradictions of sense—'is better

---

[1] Heracl. Fr. 59 [10] συμφερόμενον διαφερόμενον, συναῖδον
διαῖδον.   Cp. 46 [8] τὸ ἀντίξουν συμφέρον, καὶ ἐκ τῶν διαφερόντων
καλλίστην ἁρμονίαν.   45 [51] οὐ ξυνίασι ὅκως διαφερόμενον ἑωυτῷ
ὁμολογέει.

than the visible.'[1]   It is interesting to reflect
that one of the last of the Greek philosophers,
Plotinus (born 204 A.D.), joins hands with
Heraclitus, applying the same principle to
illustrate the harmony of contrasted elements
in a work of art, and especially in the drama.[2]
The 'rational principle of the drama is a unity'
of action, 'containing in it many collisions,'[3]
and out of this play of contraries is evolved
the harmony of the whole.   So too, he argues,
in the drama of life where the soul is the
actor, the universal reason, presiding over the
struggle, resolves the dissonance and discord
in a final harmony.   Heraclitus had already
grasped the truth of Western civilisation, that
the struggle of opposing forces—his metaphorical 'warfare' (πόλεμος)—is the condition
of progress, and that this holds good in human
society no less than in the · evolution of
the cosmic order.   This profound philosophic
truth the Greeks applied instinctively in prac-

---

[1] Heracl. Fr. 47 [54] ἁρμονίη ἀφανὴς φανερῆς κρείσσων.

[2] Plotin. *Enn.* iii. 2. 11 ff.

[3] *Ib.* iii. 2. 16 δράματος λόγος εἷς ἔχων ἐν αὐτῷ πολλὰς μάχας.

tical life.   In politics they never fell under the
fanatical sway of any single principle—not
royalty, not aristocracy, not democracy.   Here
too they sought to discover the harmony of opposites.   The friction and play of contending forces
were needed, they felt, alike for stability and
development.   The State and the Individual,
Order and Progress, Necessity and Freedom—
these permanent antagonisms of thought, were
not left, as they were in the East, to confront
one another in hostile isolation.   The contradictions, if not solved, were at least softened.
Nowhere more than in her colonial life, in
those busy and rival centres of intellect and
commerce, did Greece exhibit her versatile
power of reconciling things not previously
combined.   The new experiments struck out
in art, in philosophy, in social and political
organisation, involved a kind of mediatorial
process.   They were the product of a spirit of
adjustment, balance, compromise.   They are
the creation of the Western mind.

The temperament of the people as a whole
is a compound as remarkable as are the gifts

united in the great men of the race — a
people shrewdly practical yet sternly idealistic ;
jealous of alien influences yet hospitable to
foreigners ;   intolerant   of   unorthodoxy   yet
ready to laugh over their own pantheon ;
slaves to party spirit yet gifted with a singular
faculty of political compromise ; endowed with
a proverbial gaiety of heart, which blends,
however, with a sadness sometimes bordering
on pessimism.   The diverse and seemingly
opposite qualities which mark the Greek mind
are one secret of its matchless force, and the
cause of its success in so many fields of human
activity, practical and speculative.   They constitute the chief reason why Greek literature
speaks in so many voices, and utters its appeal
to every race and generation in its turn.
Hence comes its wealth of suggestion, its
recuperative energy, its power of perpetual
adaptation.

V

GREEK LITERARY CRITICISM [1]

IN devoting two lectures to a subject which extends over seven or eight centuries and carries us from the fifth century B.C. far into the Christian era, I propose to restrict myself to a few authors and a few points of interest.

[1] In preparing these somewhat desultory discourses (V. and VI.) I have had in mind the fact that Professor Saintsbury's *History of Criticism* (Blackwood and Sons) has now placed in the hands of English readers a systematic treatment of the whole subject. I have, therefore, confined myself to following out a few trains of thought which seemed to fall in with the general scheme of this volume. Some excuse is needed for passing so lightly over 'Longinus' *On the Sublime* (περὶ ὕψους), a critical essay of unique value and interest. The truth is, it would not be easy to add much to the admirable appreciation contained in Professor Saintsbury's chapter (vol. i. pp. 152–173) and to the handling of the treatise by Professor W. Rhys Roberts in his edition (Cambridge University Press).

The treatment will necessarily be discursive and the order not always chronological. But it may be convenient so far to follow the lines of historical development as to include in the first part of our survey mainly the criticism of Poetry, in the latter part, the criticism of Prose.

Literary criticism in Greece as a distinct and conscious art was late in its appearing. The period of creative activity was, it is true, a period also of varied critical reflection both in art and literature ; and here and there we come across writers of original genius who were critics of their own craft or of that of others. But these are rare exceptions. It is not till the time of Aristotle that we find any systematised discussion on works of literature, or on the principles that govern the literary art. Professed critics—men who write books on other books — were still unknown. The essay, the monograph, the literary study of a particular author, are a product of the post-classical age, when the centre of Greek civilisation had been shifted, and Hellenism had found a new abode first at Alexandria, and afterwards at Rome. With the 'reviewer' in the modern sense the Greek world never became acquainted.

In the poetical schools of Greece reflection had been at work and discussion rife for centuries before the Periclean era. Between master and pupil there was a constant and oral interchange of ideas. Theory and practice went hand in hand. Criticism was as yet from within ; it was, as we might say, the criticism of the workshop or the studio. Such, for instance, is the advice given to Pindar by Corinna, the Boeotian poetess : 'Sow with the hand, not with the sack.'[1] Here we have the principle of artistic parsimony, the law of reserve, the truth expressed by the Greek proverb, 'The half is greater than the whole.' In such an atmosphere of teaching and learning poetry grew up. Literary forms or types were created — epic, lyric, dramatic,

---

[1] Plut. *De Glor. Athen.* c. iv. p. 347 τῇ χειρὶ δεῖν σπείρειν ἀλλὰ μὴ ὅλῳ τῷ θυλάκῳ. For other examples see W. R. Hardie, *Lectures on Classical Subjects* (Macmillan and Co.), pp. 266-269.

elegiac—which have stood the test of time and become the accepted models of the Western world. Behind the activity of creative genius a ceaseless critical effort was at work, controlling and inspiring poetic invention. Standards of writing were formed, canons of taste laid down, and the great problem of reconciling tradition with freedom of development was in process of solution. Meanwhile the variations of literary type answered to the living forces operating in society. The poets followed close upon the movements of the race and the people. Their 'invention,' their originality, consisted chiefly in vitalising old material, in interpreting the legends in the light of the present, in re-creating and ever renewing the marvellous history of the past. To make old things seem new and new things seem familiar, was one main function of their art. Viewed in this light the critical faculty of the Greeks stood nearer to the creative imagination than moderns can easily realise. The fine gift of discrimination, the instinct of omission and rejection, the power of seizing in their own mythology the facts which had in them the kernel of poetic truths—all this formed part of the poetic equipment of the race.

In the Periclean age this creative, or re-creative, function of poetry was fulfilled more especially by the tragic drama. But what form did dramatic criticism take? Professional critics as yet there were none: but we must not infer that there was no effective criticism. The Athenians were 'nothing if not critical'; and never probably at any epoch of history were literary productions brought so directly to the bar of public opinion; a public opinion, too, that was in a sense the verdict of the State. If literary judgments were not passed daily or weekly, the decision was but the more authoritative when it came. At Athens the dramatic competitions were held twice a year, at the two great festivals of Dionysus. The judges—five in number for comedy, and probably the same number for the tragic contests—acted under solemn oath as in a court of law. They were appointed with elaborately devised pre-cautions to secure an impartial verdict. These

anonymous umpires were chosen by ballot from
a select list, and their names divulged only after
the award. A defeated competitor might question the fairness of their award by instituting
a prosecution, and the case would then be
tried before a popular tribunal. In our own
day we have seen actions for libel brought
against dramatic critics : we should like to be
better informed as to how a similar prosecution
was conducted at Athens. We read indeed of
some strange results in these competitions ; the
defeat, for instance, of the *Oedipus Tyrannus* of
Sophocles (the play which Aristotle regarded
as the model of dramatic construction) by an
obscure poet Philocles, the nephew of Aeschylus.
Still more unaccountable in the next century
was the poor success that attended Menander,
who exhibited 108 comedies, but was only
eight times victorious. Yet in most instances
our surprise would probably be lessened if we
were in possession of all the facts—if the com-
peting plays were extant for comparison, and
if, moreover, we could estimate the other factors
which both in Tragedy and the Old Comedy

counted in the award—the singing, the dancing, and the choral equipment.

We hear of but few protests against the
verdict of the judges.   In Greece at large the
Athenian judgment on tragedy seems to have
been accepted as final.   To Athens the trage-
dian looked for his credentials ; it lay with her
to set the seal of her approval on his art.   The
testimony of Plato on this head[1] agrees with
the view ascribed to Aeschylus in the *Frogs*,
that 'the rest of the world,' compared with
them 'were mere trash at judging the poetic
faculty.'[2]   He himself, it is true, had to wait
fifteen years before he won success ; but having
done so, he retained his supremacy to the
end ; and at his death poetic privileges, of a
kind then unique, were conferred on him.[3]
Sophocles, in like manner but without pre-

---

[1] *Laches* 183 A–B.

[2] *Frogs* 809-810 :

> λῆρον τε τἄλλ' ἡγεῖτο τοῦ γνῶναι πέρι
> φύσεις ποιητῶν.

[3] The Athenians passed a special decree permitting his tragedies
to compete at the Dionysia after his death; Schol. on *Frogs*, 868 :

> ὅτι ἡ ποίησις οὐχὶ συντέθηκέ μοι.

liminary failures, during a literary career of
about sixty years, held an almost undisputed
sway.   And yet there is no trace of either of
these great masters ever having lowered his
art to satisfy a vulgar taste.   They were able to
lift their hearers to their own high plane of
thought and imagination.   It was an unparal-
leled achievement.   The themes handled were
such as demanded and received ideal treatment.
The theatre was of colossal size ; the audience
a vast one, far outnumbering the gatherings of
the assembly or the law-courts ; it comprised
every grade of culture and ignorance, though
the men of culture formed but a small minority.
If Euripides fared less well at the hands of his
countrymen — his victories amounting in all
only to five — we must remember that he
generally competed against Sophocles.   After
his death the balance was redressed ; a great
and growing enthusiasm for him set in ; due,
we may suspect, not less to the love of rhetoric
which had overspread the Greek world than to
his genius, which at first had been somewhat
underrated.   Be that as it may, the critical

instinct of the public and the sureness of their literary perceptions in the fifth century is on the whole a fact as certain as it is significant.

A contemporary judgment is often reversed by posterity; examples are afforded by the literary history of almost every nation. But Time, to which Aeschylus is said to have dedicated his tragedies,[1] has not only ratified his particular claim, but in well-nigh every department of poetry, has endorsed the verdict of Athens. Aristotle had good grounds for the opinion he held as to the critical value of popular taste. While laying emphasis on the mixed elements of refinement and vulgarity of which an audience is composed,[2] he still maintains that the collective judgment of the many in æsthetic matters is superior to the judgment of any single individual.[3]

---

[1] Athen. viii. 39 χρόνῳ τὰς τραγῳδίας ἀνατιθέναι.

[2] *Pol.* v. (viii.) 7. 1342 a 18-22 ἐπεὶ δ' ὁ θεατὴς διττός, ὁ μὲν ἐλεύθερος καὶ πεπαιδευμένος, ὁ δὲ φορτικός κ.τ.λ.

[3] *Ib.* iii. 11. 1281 a 42 ff., esp. 1281 b 8-10 διὸ καὶ κρίνουσιν ἄμεινον οἱ πολλοὶ καὶ τὰ τῆς μουσικῆς ἔργα καὶ τὰ τῶν ποιητῶν· ἄλλοι γὰρ ἄλλο τι μόριον, πάντα δὲ πάντες. Cp. 1282 a 1-21, and

And we can to-day observe that what often distinguishes the verdict of an intelligent public from that of the expert critic, is a swift and immediate impression which embraces the whole instead of accentuating the parts.

Plato would not have agreed with Aristotle's view. The supreme test of artistic excellence is, he holds, the pleasure afforded to 'the one man who is pre-eminent in virtue and education.' [1] He contrasts his own age with earlier times. The judges, he says, have now fallen under the dominion of the audience;—and he coins the word θεατροκρατία to denote this idea. Instead of instructors they have become the pupils of the crowd. They have yielded to the clamour of the theatre: and the poets in turn, infected by their corruption, are obliged to humour a degenerate public.[2] It is indeed probable that popular taste underwent some weakening in the fourth century. But the contrast as drawn

iii. 15. 1286 a 30 διὸ καὶ κρίνει ἄμεινον ὄχλος πολλὰ ἢ εἷς ὁστισοῦν.

[1] *Laws* ii. 659 A ἕνα τὸν ἀρετῇ τε καὶ παιδείᾳ διαφέροντα.

[2] *Ib.* ii. 659 A—C, iii. 700 C—701 A.

by Plato is surely overstated.   The drama has
been truly called the most democratic of the
arts ; [1] and in every age when it has been a
living force, the influence of the audience has
been powerfully felt.   We cannot doubt that
in the fifth as in the fourth century the voice
of the people must often have decisively affected
the award of the judges.

The influence of the audience on the poet
is one of the points of dramatic criticism which
is touched on in the *Poetics*.[2]   The question
as to the proper ending of tragedy seems to
have been debated at the time in literary circles.
Aristotle pronounces in favour of the unhappy
ending, the other kind being, as he thinks,
appropriate only to comedy, where the bitterest
enemies walk off hand in hand at the close,—
'no one slays or is slain'; or, as Goethe says,
'no one dies, every one is married.'   But even

[1] Brander Matthews, *The Development of the Drama* (New
York), p. 33.   This volume traces in a very interesting way the
influence which the audience, the actors, and the size and construction of the theatre exert on the form of the drama.

[2] *Poet.* xiii. 6-8.   See Butcher, *Aristotle's Theory of Poetry
and Fine Art* (third ed.), p. 305 ff.

in tragedy, Aristotle observes, the happy ending is commonly preferred 'owing to the weakness of the audience' (διὰ τὴν θεάτρων ἀσθένειαν). People are not robust enough to endure the painful conclusion ; so the poet against his better judgment yields to the liking for melo-drama. 'We have all,' as some one has said, 'a secret *penchant* for false sentiment.' The craving for 'poetic justice,' the morbidly moral desire to make things come right on the stage, all the more because they are so apt to go wrong in life, is only one example of an instinct, amiable but prosaic, to which the play-going public is always liable.

Criticism in the form of public opinion, direct and effective as it was at Athens, is not in strictness literary criticism. Literary criti-cism proper spoke for the first time through the lips of comedy. Unlike tragedy, comedy in the fifth century B.C. had its life in the present ; it reflected the spirit of the day ; its allusions were local ; its topics were current events, politics, literature. The comic poet was not only author, stage-manager, ballet-

master, musician, and sometimes actor, but
wielded an office which combined in some
degree functions similar to those exercised by
Punch, the old *Saturday Review*, and the
Comic Opera.   As an organ of literary criticism the Aristophanic comedy dealt mainly
with the productions of the tragic stage.   Nor
was it enough for the comic poet to be witty
or scathing ; as a critic of poetry he must
himself be a master of the poetic art, and able
to hold his own beside the great tragedians
themselves.   In the *Frogs* of Aristophanes,
Aeschylus and Euripides, as rival candidates
for the throne of poetry, are placed upon the
stage.   Each argues his own cause and cari-
catures the manner of his opponent.   It is
the earliest instance we possess of literary
criticism in the form of parody, and probably
the most brilliant example of the kind in all
literature.   In this as in other plays Aristophanes vindicates his claim to be a critic by
proving himself a consummate craftsman in
every style of poetic composition ; while in
lyrical utterance, his notes are among the

purest and most melodious that have flowed from any Greek singer.

We cannot here discuss the justice of the Aristophanic criticism or the value of his reflections on the art of poetry. But two observations may be made in passing. First, in the linguistic attacks made on Euripides he touches with playful irony that love of verbal subtlety, of fine-drawn distinctions, the

> Quibbling, counter-quibbling, prating,
> Argufying and debating,

to which the Greeks were always addicted, and which, when the genius of the race was exhausted, ended in the arid disputations of Byzantine schoolmen. Secondly, Aristophanes is still at the standpoint of the early Greek world ; he assumes that poetry has a didactic aim ; the poet is the moral teacher of the community, the educator of grown men ; it is he that inspires them with courage and civic loyalty :

> Children and boys have a teacher assigned them,—
> The bard is a master for manhood and youth,

> Bound to instruct them in virtue and truth,
> Beholden and bound.[1]

These words are put into the mouth of
Aeschylus. But they are tacitly accepted by
Euripides, who admits the duty of good
counsel (χρηστὰ λέγειν, χρηστὰ διδάσκειν),
merely insisting that it should be conveyed ' in
the language of men ' (ἀνθρωπείως φράζειν), not
couched in the grandiloquent style of his rival.
Already the question had been put to him :

> Tell me then what are the principal merits
> Entitling a poet to praise and renown ?

and he had replied :

> The improvement of morals, the progress of mind,
> When a poet by skill and invention
> Can render his audience virtuous and wise. [2]

By Euripides' own confession it is the glory of
poetry that it ' makes men better ' ; though,

---

[1] Frere's Trans. of *Frogs* 1054-1056 :

> τοῖς μὲν γὰρ παιδαρίοισιν
> ἔστι διδάσκαλος ὅστις φράζει, τοῖσιν δ' ἡβῶσι ποιηταί.
> πάνυ δὴ δεῖ χρηστὰ λέγειν ἡμᾶς.

[2] Frere's Trans. of *Frogs* 1008-1010 :

> ΑΙΣ. ἀπόκριναί μοι, τίνος οὕνεκα χρὴ θαυμάζειν ἄνδρα ποιητήν ;
> ΕΥ. δεξιότητος καὶ νουθεσίας, ὅτι βελτίους τε ποιοῦμεν
>   τοὺς ἀνθρώπους ἐν ταῖς πόλεσιν κ.τ.λ.

doubtless, the phrase would not bear quite the same meaning to him as to Aeschylus. And if the citizens, once good men and true, have been debased by him, he deserves, Dionysus says, 'to die'; and he himself does not dissent. This attitude of mind was at once the strength and the weakness of Greek poetical criticism : its strength because it kept alive the idea that art and poetry are not merely the private delight of the individual; they belong to the community; they are the expression of its moral and spiritual life : a source, again, of weakness, inasmuch as the poets came to be thought of as moralists. They were expected to yield edifying lessons outside their art ; and if their utterances could not be wrested to the desired end, adverse sentence was too often passed upon them.

The vein of parody which runs through the Aristophanic drama and appears to have been a marked feature of the Old Comedy, was imitated and developed in the next generation. For sixty or seventy years after the death of Aristophanes comedy was a frequent

vehicle of indirect literary criticism. The
interest, however, of these later *jeux d'esprit*,
so far as we can judge from the surviving
fragments, lies less in their suggestive or
critical value than in the acquaintance they
seem to imply on the part of the audience
with the poetical literature of Greece. Tragedians and lyrical writers all came under con-
tribution. Whole scenes from tragedy were
travestied. The manner or diction of particular authors was reproduced. Quotations
and reminiscences were strewn broadcast
through the plays. The popular love of
literary parody, combined with certain com-
pliments (surely half ironical) addressed to
the audience by the comic poets, has led some
scholars to infer the existence of a large
reading public at Athens in the fifth and
fourth centuries B.C.[1] The evidence, however,
is far from supporting this view. Actual illiter-
ates, doubtless, were rare. But there is a great

---

[1] E.g. *Frogs* 1109-1118: esp. 1114:

βιβλίον τ' ἔχων ἕκαστος μανθάνει τὰ δεξιά,

where βιβλίον seems to be the 'libretto' or book of the words.

array of facts to show that the bulk of the
people can have had little or no direct acquaintance with books.   And not only was there no
diffused literary culture in the stricter sense, but
the mass of the audience at the theatre were
not even familiar with their own mythology.
There is a startling sentence in the *Poetics*
which is too explicit to be set aside : 'The
known legends are known only to a few.' [1]

So far as the audience were acquainted
with tragic poetry, it was from stage representation, not through reading.   Yet we cannot
on that account assume any lack of a literary
sense.   Indeed, it is probably true that under
certain conditions, an instinctive good taste,
which has been cultivated by listening to oral
literature, is merely deadened or impaired by
book learning.   In any case, at Athens, however narrow may have been the range of their
culture, the people had an exquisite feeling
for words and appreciation of the musical
capacities of speech.   When Gorgias made

---

[1] *Poet.* ix. 8 ἐπεὶ καὶ τὰ γνώριμα ὀλίγοις γνώριμά ἐστιν ἀλλ'
ὅμως εὐφραίνει πάντας.

his first appearance among them, we are told
that the striking novelty of his diction came
with a pleasurable shock on the sensitive ears
of the audience.[1] In political debate and in
the administration of justice this æsthetic
sensibility was a danger of which the Athenians
themselves were aware ; and it would seem
that there was a special nickname for persons
who were thus fooled by the pleasure of the
ear.[2] But a fine and trained instinct for
language was the very condition which made
it possible for the average Athenian, unversed
in books, to become a capable critic even of
the higher poetry. Add to this a marvellous
alertness of mind, a power of catching a point
or seeing an allusion, which is vouched for
by the most various testimony, and which
justified Demosthenes in declaring : ' No people

---

[1] Diodor. xii. 53 καὶ τῷ ξενίζοντι τῆς λέξεως ἐξέπληξε τοὺς
'Αθηναίους ὄντας εὐφυεῖς καὶ φιλολόγους.

[2] See Eustath. 1522, 26 " ὦ μόνοι ὦτοι τῶν 'Ελλήνων " (a quota-
tion from comedy), and the explanation 1687, 60 οἱ ῥᾷον ὑπὸ τοῦ
τυχόντος ἐξαπατώμενοι ὦτοι ἐλέγοντο, προσφυέστερον δὲ ἂν ὦτοι
καλοῦντο οἱ ἐκ μόνης ἀκοῆς ἀπεριέργως καὶ ἀνεξετάστως ἀπάτην
πάσχοντες. The word meant literally a ' horned owl,' hence a
' booby.'

is so quick at taking a speaker's meaning.' [1]

With such intellectual gifts, aided also
by the art of the actor—his gestures and
declamation—the regular theatre-goer would
at once recognise on the comic stage the tone
and diction of tragedy, the familiar manner
of its dialogue or choral songs, and would
flatter himself on his own discovery. It
mattered not if only a few could identify the
lines that were quoted or adapted, and assign
them to their proper sources.[2] Even the
scenes that were travestied might not to the
ordinary hearer suggest the originals, except
in those rare instances—some of which are
known to us—where the play from which the
parody was drawn had been recently exhibited. The comedian, after all, aimed only
at a broad effect. He counted, and not in

[1] *Ol.* iii. 15 γνῶναι πάντων ὑμεῖς ὀξύτατοι τὰ ῥηθέντα.

[2] Cp. Diphilus ii. Fr. 73 κ: some lines are quoted from
Euripides, and one speaker asks,

πόθεν ἐστὶ ταῦτα πρὸς θεῶν ;

The other replies,

τί δέ σοι μέλει ;

οὐ γὰρ τὸ δρᾶμα, τὸν δὲ νοῦν σκοπούμεθα.

vain, on a general and keen appreciation of
literary style. It was enough for him if the
mass of the audience took the main point.
There was always an inner circle who would
delight in the subtler turns of phrase and
the associations which the parody called
up.

All this, however, is literary criticism of the
indirect kind,—though characteristically Attic
in its very indirectness and allusiveness. In
Plato we have the first beginnings of the large,
the philosophic criticism which views literature
as one of the ideal expressions of the human
spirit, and seeks to arrive at the innermost laws
of the art. Yet Plato seldom speaks of literary
productions except in a tone of apology and
distrust. Himself the greatest artist in prose
that has ever lived, he was apt to think of the
written word as dead, mechanical, irresponsive,
standing before you with the cold beauty of a
graven image, but helpless for self - defence,
wanting in flexibility and adjustment.[1] Literature, if it is to be of any worth at all, must be

---

[1] *Phaedr.* 275 D–E.

the image of the animated word,[1] a living force,
engendering life and moulding character. This
it can only be if it is planted in a congenial
soul, whence to other souls can be transmitted
a fruitful and immortal seed of thought. It
must come in the spirit and power of philosophy,
not as a doctrine but as a quickening influence.
The φιλόλογος must himself be φιλόσοφος.
This it was that determined Plato's view of
the relation in which literature stands to life.
To do things worthy to be written was in his
eyes a dignity higher than to write things
worthy to be read. A noble life is the noblest
drama : the maker or artist who can teach us
to build up such a life is the best of poets.[2]
The words of Milton, at once Hellenist and
Hebraist, come to our memory : ' He who
would not be frustrate of his hope to write well
hereafter in laudable things, ought himself to be

---

[1] *Phaedr.* 276 A τὸν τοῦ εἰδότος λόγον λέγεις ζῶντα καὶ
ἔμψυχον, οὗ ὁ γεγραμμένος εἴδωλον ἄν τι λέγοιτο δικαίως.

[2] *Laws* vii. 817 B ἡμεῖς ἐσμὲν τραγῳδίας αὐτοὶ ποιηταὶ κατὰ
δύναμιν ὅ τι καλλίστης ἅμα καὶ ἀρίστης· πᾶσα οὖν ἡμῖν ἡ
πολιτεία ξυνέστηκε μίμησις τοῦ καλλίστου καὶ ἀρίστου βίου, ὃ
δή φαμεν ἡμεῖς γε ὄντως εἶναι τραγῳδίαν τὴν ἀληθεστάτην.

a true poem, that is, a composition and pattern of the best and honourablest things.' As against this we may set the remark of a modern writer : 'A fine book is the end for which the world was made.'

Of the great ideas which Plato has contributed to literary criticism the greatest are to be found in the *Phaedrus*. We have already alluded to the theory there set forth of poetic inspiration.[1] Two other ideas may here be noted. In the first place, at the root of all good writing lies sincerity of conviction. The writer must have something to say, and must say it at first-hand. Where there is nothing to express there can be no artistic beauty, for the essence of the literary art is that it shall express reality. 'It is no genuine art of words that he will have who does not know the truth of things, but has tried to hunt out what other people think about it.'[2] Hence the uselessness of mere mechanical rules. All the 'ologies' and technical terms of the rhetoricians will not teach you to speak or write well. When once a true

Supr. p. 143 ff. [2] *Phaedr.* 262 c.

idea is strongly conceived, the 'irresistible law
of right utterance' (λογογραφικὴ ἀνάγκη)[1] will
follow.   The second principle, closely related to
the first, is that an artistic composition is an
organic whole.   'It must in its structure be
like a living thing, with head, feet, and body ;
there must be a middle and extremities, the
parts being adapted to one another and to the
whole.'[2]

Here, observe, and for the first time, the law
of internal unity is enunciated as a primary
condition of literary art—now a commonplace,
then a discovery.[3]   The thought was taken up
by Aristotle and became the basis of his reasoning on the drama.   Organic as distinct from
mechanical unity ; not the homogeneous same-
ness of a sand-heap, but a unity combined with
variety, a unity vital and structural, implying
mutual interdependence of all the parts, such
that if one part is displaced or removed the

---

[1] *Phaedr.* 264 B.   [2] *Ib.* 264 C.

[3] Plato applies this principle of organic unity to the moral
government of the world in the *Laws* x. 903 B–C, where all the
parts are said to be ordered with a view to the excellence of the
whole.

whole is dislocated—that is the leading critical idea of the *Poetics*.[1]   From this point of view the unity and artistic beauty of a literary composition are found to reside in a pervasive harmony, a dominant impression, a single animating and controlling principle.   So said the Greeks and so we say.   But every people has not shared this view.   'In the Persian ode,' says Mr. Leaf (in his introduction to *Versions from Hafiz*), 'we find a succession of couplets often startling in their independence. . . . To the Persian each couplet is a whole in itself, . . . sufficiently beautiful if it be adequately expressed, and not of necessity owing anything to that which comes before or after.   It is from the common metre and common rhyme alone that the ode gains a formal unity.   As Eastern poets are never tired of telling us, the making of an ode is the threading of pearls upon a string ; the couplet is the pearl, round and smooth and perfect in itself, the metre is but the thread which binds them all together.' This is very unlike the law of unity as under-

---

[1] *Poet*. viii. 4 ; cp. xxiii. 1.

O

stood by the Greeks. To them the dominant impression of oneness, the feeling of the whole, both in prose and poetry, seemed so indispensable that even in historical composition they shrank from admitting actual records, speeches, treaties, letters, or the like—anything which even in style might seem to mar the narrative by crossing it with a thing of alien texture.

Moderns, however, while accepting the Greek principle of unity as a primary requirement of art, have not in their judgments on Greek literature always accepted it in the Greek sense. Unity they demand, but another unity than that which satisfied the Greeks. They often fail to take account of the varying degrees of unity appropriate to the different forms of literature. Within the spacious compass of the Epic, as Aristotle pointed out,[1] ampler episodes may be admitted and a more discursive freedom allowed than is possible in the close and serried sequence of the drama. And it may be observed that, while in antiquity captious critics discovered all

[1] *Poet.* xviii. 4 ; xxiii. 3 ; xxiv. 4.

manner of flaws in Homer, one defect alone
they never discovered—a want of unity in the
Iliad or the *Odyssey*. Indeed, according to
Aristotle, it is the unity of these poems that
constitutes their pre-eminent excellence, a unity
derived not from the hero being one but from
the action being one.[1] ' In structure they are
as perfect as possible ; each is, in the highest
degree attainable, an imitation of a single
action.'[2] The Platonic dialogues are another
case in point. Several strands of thought are
here subtly interwoven. In the *Phaedrus*—the
very dialogue in which the stringent law of
unity is prescribed — where does the unity
reside ? What is the real subject of the
dialogue ? Is it love, as treated in the earlier
part, or rhetoric which is treated later, or something larger than either of these ? So too in
the *Republic*, what is its theme ? The dialogue
reaches beyond the nature of Justice, or the
constitution of the ideal State. Only by degrees
do we come to see how delicate are the links
which bind a single Platonic dialogue into a

[1] *Poet*. viii. 1-3.   [2] *Poet*. xxvi. 6.

whole, and how the apparently disconnected topics may be merged in a higher unity. Here is no want of art, but an art so finished as to elude our rough and often mechanical tests. It should serve as a warning to certain modern critics to whom ancient masterpieces appear to be the work of ' a committee with power to add to their numbers.'

We pass now to the *Poetics* of Aristotle, the only piece of systematic criticism—and yet how unsystematic—that has come down to us from the classical age of Greece. A strange irony it seems that the most severely logical and, in a sense, unimaginative of philosophers should have seen more deeply into the inner nature of poetry than Plato, who of all philosophers was most poetical ; and that the *Poetics*, a fragmentary and tentative treatise, which in many respects is the spirit of prose incarnate, should have permanently affected the poetical theories of Europe. No ancient treatise, however, has so philosophic an outlook on literature, such precision in detail, such wealth of suggestion, so many remarks far-reaching in their scope and dropped with such careless and lavish ease. In proportion as we are able to rid ourselves of old misapprehensions, to discard the glosses of half-instructed expositors, and to read the book in the light of Aristotle's own system, the more profound does his teaching appear.

We could wish, indeed, that he had taken to heart the words of Plato: 'Whoso knocks at the doors of Poesy untouched by the Muses' frenzy, fondly persuading himself that art alone will make him a thorough poet, neither he nor his works will ever attain perfection, but are destined for all their cold propriety to be eclipsed by the effusions of the inspired madman.'[1] That Aristotle did not entirely ignore the 'ecstatic' element in poetry we have already seen.[2] But while aware of the existence of the inspired poet, of whom Plato tells in the *Phaedrus* and the *Ion*, he writes of

---

[1] *Phaedr.* 245 A ὃς δ' ἂν ἄνευ μανίας Μουσῶν ἐπὶ ποιητικὰς θύρας ἀφίκηται, πεισθεὶς ὡς ἄρα ἐκ τέχνης ἱκανὸς ποιητὴς ἐσόμενος, ἀτελὴς αὐτός τε καὶ ἡ ποίησις ὑπὸ τῆς τῶν μαινομένων ἡ τοῦ σωφρονοῦντος ἠφανίσθη. (Trans. W. H. Thompson.)

[2] Supr. p. 146.

poetry in too coldly logical a manner, as if its emotional effects could be attained by following rules of dramatic construction, by orderly arrangement and analysis. We could wish, again, that he had shown more appreciation of the grandeur of Aeschylus; of the humour and unquenchable laughter of Aristophanes; that he had not passed over with deliberate neglect (for such it would seem to be) the great lyrical poetry of Greece—Simonides, Pindar, Sappho, Alcaeus, to none of whom does he make even faint allusion. True, the treatise is a fragment; but there are good grounds for thinking that this does not account for the fact. Was it, perhaps, that lyrical poetry interested him only as a rudimentary art—uttering itself in the form of improvised chants and dithyrambic hymns—which marked a stage in the development of the drama? for in the drama, he held, the poetic art culminated; even the epic being treated by him as imperfectly developed drama. May it not also be that in the personal outbursts of lyrical song, in the self-abandonment, the rush of feeling of Sappho

or Alcaeus, he missed the characteristic Hellenic
self-restraint—this unimpassioned critic, who
appears, moreover, to have been but little
susceptible to the magic of words and the
charm of musical speech ? Yet all this does
not explain his omission of Pindar. In any
case, we have here certain limitations of his
poetic sensibility, and of a kind so striking
that they should not pass unnoticed.

Still, when all deductions have been made,
the permanent value of the book increases the
more it is studied. Its strength lies in this,
that Aristotle had before him a literature of
wonderful range and originality ; that the laws
presiding over its creation were not the
arbitrary rules of a school, but, we may almost
say, the artistic laws of the human mind ; and
that he arrives at his principles by a penetrating
power of observation and analysis, and a wide
induction drawn from the practice of the great
writers. And, throughout the inquiry, he
maintains that attitude of judicial impartiality
which he himself, in one of his physical
writings, notes as a mark of the true critical

spirit : 'We should be umpires and not litigants.'[1]

It has been sometimes said that Aristotle thinks only of the form—the artistic form— not of the content of poetry. But this appears to be a misapprehension. Perhaps the most original and pregnant saying in the *Poetics* is that which declares poetry to be 'a more philosophic and higher thing than history,' being concerned with the universal not with the particular.[2] It tells of what man does or may do in given circumstances ; of the permanent possibilities of human nature as distinct from the acts of the individual—'what Alcibiades did or suffered.' The subject-matter of poetry is the universal—that which is abiding and structural in humanity, which appeals to all men and finds a response in every age. Poetry is not, as some modern writers would have us believe, interested only or chiefly in the rare and unique case, in some abnormal fact of

---

[1] *De Caelo* i. 10. 279 b 11 δεῖ διαιτητὰς ἀλλ' οὐκ ἀντιδίκους εἶναι.

[2] *Poet.* ix. 3 διὸ καὶ φιλοσοφώτερον καὶ σπουδαιότερον ποίησις ἱστορίας ἐστίν.

psychology,—or rather, we should perhaps say, of pathology. But here comes the point I desire to emphasise. Unity of form is brought by Aristotle into immediate and even necessary connexion with universality of content.[1] The one depends on the other. In proportion as the subject-matter is universalised, the unity is perfected. For in the process of universalising, the transient and perishable part is eliminated ; the unreason of chance is expelled ; we are admitted to observe the working of human motive in a world into which pure accident hardly intrudes, where cause and effect have fuller and freer play—the realm of art which is a realm of design. In short, the world of poetry — and this is true pre-eminently of dramatic poetry — is a world more unified, more intelligible than the world of experience, just because the subject-matter is the universal.

No other ancient writer, so far as I know, has hinted at this close relation between artistic

---

[1] Chap. viii. of the *Poetics* deals with artistic unity, chap. ix. with universalised subject-matter, and the opening words mark the connexion,—φανερὸν δὲ ἐκ τῶν εἰρημένων.

unity and universality of content. Lesser
critics have been always disposed to think of
form and subject - matter apart, and to lay
emphasis on one to the neglect of the other.
But in Aristotle the two things are as inseparable in the higher kinds of imaginative
literature as they are in his philosophy. The
first principle of his philosophic system is
that the union of form and matter, of εἶδος
and ὕλη, is necessary to make the real, the
concrete object. To separate them in philosophy is to reduce philosophic thought to mere
abstractions. To separate them in literature is
the direct negation of all that artistic production implies. Literature becomes either, on
the one hand, formless and chaotic, or, on the
other, devoid of reality, out of touch with life.

Aristotle's remarks often contain an implicit
reply to objections which had been urged by
Plato. Let us take a single point by way of
illustration. It touches a problem which vexed
the mind and conscience of Greece throughout
its history. Plato in his dialogues wavers
between his awe and love of Homer, ' the

wisest of our poets,'[1] 'the captain and teacher
of that charming tragic company,'[2] and a still
more passionate love of truth.   Fascinated
though he is by Homer's genius he cannot
admit him to his ideal republic.   Homer 'tells
lies,' and lies too that are immoral.[3]   His
gods and men do things which ought neither to
be done nor heard of.   And whereas the aim
of poetry should be to teach us to be good and
brave and true, Homer by his potent spells
steals away our hearts.   He sets before us
weeping heroes in all the luxury of woe.   He
feeds emotions which ought to be starved, and
makes anarchy in the soul.[4]   To which Aristotle's answer on the lines of the *Poetics* would
be to this effect.   First, as to the 'lies.'   Homer
is the great master of the art of 'lying.'   He has
shown all other poets 'how to tell lies as they
ought'; he has taught them the art of beautiful
fiction.[5]   But the poet's lie is not the lie of

---

[1] *Laws* vi. 776 E.   [2] *Rep.* x. 595 C.

[3] *Rep.* ii. 377 D–E.   [4] *Rep.* x. 606 A–D.

[5] *Poet.* xxiv. 9 δεδίδαχεν δὲ μάλιστα Ὅμηρος καὶ τοὺς ἄλλους
ψευδῆ λέγειν ὡς δεῖ.   See *Aristotle's Theory of Poetry and Fine
Art* (third ed.), p. 171 ff.

common life, even as the truth of poetry stands
far apart from the truth of fact. The poet
at the outset asks you to grant him certain
assumptions which are the necessary conditions
of imaginative creation. You make your tacit
compact with him ; you accept his premisses ;
and forthwith he transports you into an ideal
world, remote from the world of experience.
In that world 'probable impossibilities' (ἀδύνατα
εἰκότα) are preferred to 'possible improb-
abilities' (δυνατὰ ἀπίθανα).[1] The things that
never were or will be, if but the poet has the
skill to lend them the air of likelihood, the
colour and the form of truth, are better—yes,
'truer' in a poetic sense—than the anomalies
of experience, the 'improbable possibilities,'
which people defend in fiction by saying, 'Oh,
but the thing happened.'

And through this emancipating word of
Aristotle's the poet, as by a touch of his
wand, can at once throw open to us the
whole world of fabulous adventure in epic
and romance, not only the wonders of the

---

[1] *Poet.* xxiv. 10 ; xxv. 17.

Odyssey, but also the fairyland of the *Arabian Nights*.

So much for the 'lies,'—Aristotle would continue. Then as to the 'immorality.' Do you not mistake the true end of poetry when you demand that it should directly teach morals? The aim of poetry is pleasure, not edification or moral instruction. Ethical principles, pure and simple, cannot be taken as the test of rightness in the domain of art. Poetry is not morals or politics any more than it is science, history, or philosophy.[1] Yet though moral and æsthetic laws are not interchangeable, let it not be thought that poetry is thereby severed entirely from morality. For pleasures differ in kind—in quality as well as in degree—and the higher the poetry,—the more elevated, the more moral, will be the pleasure. The pleasure which is the aim of art cannot be produced by the representation of the morally ignoble or depraved. Some things are unfit for art—too trivial, too hideous, too squalid. In tragedy, nobility of character is necessary to awaken the

---

[1] *Poet.* xxv. 3.

blended emotions of pity and fear. Wicked-
ness is admissible only when demanded by an
inner necessity in the evolution of the action,
by the cogent requirement of dramatic motive.[1]
Even the bad persons permitted in comedy are
not absolutely bad. Their badness consists in
an ugliness or deformity of character which is
painless, and therefore can be ludicrous.[2]
Degraded lives there are in nature, but that is
no reason for reproducing them simply as
degraded in art. For art has to do not with
the ideally worse, but with the ideally better—
that ' better part' (τὸ βέλτιον) to which nature
moves, though thwarted in her movement.[3]
It is not the function of art to exhibit selected
specimens of disease or decay, but to correct
nature's failures, to create such things as nature
strives to produce, to carry them to a more
perfect completion.

While art, therefore, must not be asked to
teach morals, its business being to yield pleasure,
yet incidentally it will in a sense instruct and

---

[1] *Poet.* xxv. 19.   [2] *Poet.* v. 1.
[3] See *Aristotle's Theory of Poetry and Art*, p. 151 ff.

edify by the nobility of the pleasure arising
from its ideal creations. Nor is this pleasure,
this emotional delight at which poetry aims, a
purely individual sensation. It is a pleasure
which must be tested by reference to the social
organism; it is, in a word, the higher and
enduring pleasure of the community, or of that
refined portion of it which may be taken as the
æsthetic representative of the whole. Judge
Homer's morality by this standard. Ask not
whether this or that action is in itself good or
bad, but how it fits into the general framework
of the poem; what is the dominant impression
left? Is the resultant pleasure low or is it
elevated? Does Homer indeed enfeeble the
spirit and relax the moral fibre? or does he
brace the mind to all strenuous and noble
action?

The answer which Aristotle would have
given to this question accords with the popular
conviction of Greece, a conviction which survived into the Christian era. In an imaginary
conversation by a Greek writer of the empire,
Alexander the Great, still a youth, is asked by

his father, why he reads only Homer to the neglect of all other poets, and his reply is : 'It is not every kind of poetry, just as it is not every kind of dress, that is fitting for a king ; and the poetry of Homer is the only poetry that I see to be truly noble and splendid and royal, and fit for one who will some day rule over men.'[1]

Had the principles of the *Poetics* been grasped by the successors of Aristotle, Homeric criticism and the criticism of poetry generally might have run another course. But ancient prejudice was too strong. Homer paid the penalty of his greatness. He had long been regarded as the inspired bard. He was also the universal sage, from whom could be learned the facts of history and geography and all the special arts and sciences. Then, when his information proved incorrect, there were critics who said that he 'told lies.' Yet the *Iliad* and the *Odyssey* continued to hold their own as popular manuals of conduct ; and it was precisely in his capacity of educator of youth that

[1] Dio Chrys. *Or*. ii. ad init.

Homer was most sharply attacked. The philosophers protested against his theology, the protest dating back to the sixth century B.C. ; nor was the feud between philosophy and poetry ever quite healed. Various efforts at reconciliation were made. One such attempt, well-meaning but futile, was destined to be the bane of criticism for centuries to come. Homer, it was said, must not be interpreted literally. He spoke in dark sayings. Beneath the outward narrative hidden meanings (ὑπόνοιαι) may be discovered. His stories are symbolical either of moral truths or of physical phenomena. ' Homer,' said a Stoic philosopher of the first century A.D., ' would certainly be impious if he were not allegorical.'

The influence of this vicious critical method, and the vitality of the heresy on which it rests, may be seen at their worst in the traditional interpretation of Scripture. Biblical criticism up to a recent date has been marked by many of the faults with which we are familiar in the interpretation of Homer—the violence done to the language, the neglect of the context, the

P

explaining away of contradictions, the far-fetched symbolism, the indifference to time and place, to the thought of the age and the circumstances of the writers. These defects do not merely mark the outbreak of a recurrent disease to which the human intellect is liable. The Old Testament scriptures presented moral difficulties analogous to those which had offended the Greek philosophers. Jews like Philo (first century A.D.), and Christian writers such as Clement of Alexandria and Origen (both of the third century), who were versed in Greek learning, met these difficulties by resorting to the allegorical solution, the doctrine of the hidden meaning ; and the form in which their arguments are couched betray the school of criticism whence they are derived. The writers are working on the lines of the old Homeric apologists whose theories had long ago been discredited both by Plato and Aristotle. There is no more curious example of the persistent influence of a faulty method, mischievous in its first application, doubly pernicious when extended from the secular sphere into that of religion.

Reverting for a moment to Homer we may take note of another and equally misguided line of Homeric criticism, which was already in vogue in the third and second centuries B.C. The predecessors of Aristarchus in the school of Alexandria loved to discover some 'impropriety' (ἀπρεπές) in the poet. The Homeric scholia abound in examples. In *Odyssey* xi. 524 Odysseus narrates the story of the Trojan horse within which he and his comrades were concealed : ' The charge of all was laid on me both to open the door of our close ambush and to shut the same.' These lines, says the scholiast, must be deleted ' as unseemly ' (ὡς ἀπρεπῆ) : ' that is the work of a hall-porter ' (θυρωροῦ γὰρ ἔργον). The rules of etiquette observed in the court of the Ptolemies presumably hold good for the interior of the Trojan horse. Again, in *Odyssey* xv. 82 Menelaus promises to speed his guest Telemachus on his way : ' I too will go with thee and lead thee to the towns of men, and none shall send us away empty, but will give us some one thing at least.' A note is here appended, probably from the hand of Aristophanes of Byzantium (circ. 200 B.C.): 'Again it is unseemly that Menelaus should teach Telemachus to be a mendicant.' No wonder, then, that it is also 'unseemly' for Aphrodite to set a chair for Helen (*Il.* iii. 422), and for Athene to bear a lamp to light the way for Odysseus and Telemachus (*Od.* xix. 34). 'A menial and most trivial conception' (δουλο-πρεπὲς καὶ λίαν εὐτελὲς τὸ τῆς διανοίας) is the comment we find on the latter passage.

Aristarchus, the great critic of Alexandria (circ. 170 B.C.), almost alone among the learned men of that day, brought genius and common sense to bear on the Homeric poems. His guiding principle was that Homer must be explained by himself. The Epic language was a thing apart; it must be studied in detail; Homeric and Attic usages of words must be distinguished. Again, the manners and the customs, the civilisation of other times must not be imported into the Homeric age. The method of allegory should not be applied to the Homeric mythology. The legends must be accepted in their literal sense as belonging to

the childhood of the race, without making
Homer responsible for their truth or their
morality.

Full justice has always been done to
Aristarchus as a verbal critic of Homer. But
he deserves no less credit for the vigorous war
he waged against absurdities such as those
which have been quoted. Yet, unfortunately,
he himself falls at times into the same error.
The atmosphere of Alexandria clings to him.
He cannot keep himself at the true angle of
vision and frankly accept the simplicity of
Homeric life. In *Odyssey* vi. 244 Nausicaa, on
first meeting with the shipwrecked Odysseus,
utters the wish : ' Would that such a one might
be called my husband, dwelling here, and that
it might please him here to abide ! ' To
Aristarchus the wish appeared indecorous and
unmaidenly. A little later *(Od.* vii. 311)
Alcinous exclaims : ' Would that so goodly a
man as thou art and like-minded with me, thou
wouldest wed my daughter and be called my
son-in-law, here abiding ! ' Again the critic's
sound principles fail him ; that is not how

marriages were made in the court of the
Ptolemies. He therefore rejects (ἀθετεῖ) the
verses containing Nausicaa's unmaidenly wish,
and places his mark of doubt (διστάζει) against
the six lines that tell of Alcinous' offer of
marriage. But he has some misgivings. The
lines, he admits, have a Homeric flavour ; still
they can hardly be genuine ; for who would
think of engaging his daughter to a stranger
of whom he knew nothing, and who moreover
had not even asked for her hand ?[1] In a
similar spirit of deference to the usages of
polite society Aristarchus is offended by the
passage in *Iliad* ix. 322, where the envoys
from Agamemnon took a meal in the tent of
Achilles, and ' put away the desire ' (ἐξ ἔρον ἔντο)
' of meat and drink,'—though they had already
' drunk as much as their heart desired ' (ix. 177)
before leaving the tent of Agamemnon. It
would have been better, said Aristarchus, if the
poet had written, ' again tasted ' food (ἂψ ἐπά-
σαντο)—making them take merely a light refec-

[1] See also Plutarch's guarded comments on the incident (*de
Aud. Poet.* ch. viii. p. 23).

tion out of compliment to their host.   Still from
excessive caution (ὑπὸ περιττῆς εὐλαβείας) he
did not change the reading.

Here we may take a rapid glance backwards
and observe the contrast between Alexandria
of the second century B.C. and Athens of the
fifth century B.C.

In Alexandria we have the famous Museum,
a royal foundation, with corporate rights and
large endowments, specially designed to en-
courage learning and research.   Among its other
functions it aspires to maintain the purity of
Greek idiom, to arrest the encroachments of
other tongues, and to fix a standard of taste.
To this city erudite men resort from all parts
of the world.   The accumulated treasures of
Greek literature have here found a home.   There
are two libraries containing some five or six
hundred thousand volumes.   A vast apparatus
of learning ; and with what result ? I speak
now only of the effect on literary taste and
literary criticism ; for no one could think
slightingly of the services rendered us by that
encyclopædic industry, above all by the

laborious collection and comparison of Greek texts ;—to those scholars we largely owe it that we have a Greek literature to-day. But if criticism implies some intuition and sympathy, a faculty for apprehending a writer's inmost meaning, most of their critical work, at least in the domain of poetry, is unilluminating ;—save where we meet with the sane and vigorous intelligence of Aristarchus, or discover the too rare relics and jottings of Aristotelian tradition. Even from the lighter recreations of this society of *savants*, we learn something of their quality. We read of literary symposia where erudite garrulity loved to amuse itself with questions trivial to ask, impossible to answer——Why did Nausicaa wash her garments in sea-water rather than in the river ? how could Poseidon have had so ugly a son as the Cyclops ? on which hand, the right or the left, was Aphrodite wounded by Diomede ?

Now turn from the cosmopolitan city of learning to Athens of the Periclean age. Few books, an oral literature, a diffused intellectual atmosphere, the sway of the living word,

criticism keen but unformulated. There, for
one brief moment, literature and art responded
with prompt impression to the call of patriotism
and religion ; each new product of genius made
its immediate appeal to a concourse of assembled
citizens ; and by a rare and happy fortune the
verdict of the few coincided with the instinct
of the many. The secret of the surprising
change—what was it ? Literature at Alexandria
was divorced from life ; it had become the craft
of a *coterie*, carried on within closed walls ;
ingenious, finished, industrious, sometimes even
tender and beautiful ; but no longer the
spontaneous expression of the mind of the
community. No 'current of national life was
stirring to vivify its failing force. Nor with
the waning of the creative impulse did the
critical faculty awaken—as it has done at some
periods of history—to prepare the way for
another forward movement. The critics pored
over their classic books, but as erudite men,
not as lovers of literature—πολυμαθεῖς not
φιλόλογοι. The links were broken which
bound the present in historic sympathy to the

past; and many generations were destined to elapse before it was discovered that the task of criticism demands not only learning but directness of vision, some sense of perspective, and an effort of imaginative reconstruction.

VI

GREEK LITERARY CRITICISM

'LITERATURE,' said Goethe, 'is the fragment of fragments. The smallest part of what has been done and spoken is recorded, and the smallest part of what has been recorded has survived.' May we not add, from the Greek point of view,—'the smallest part of what has survived is literature'? The modern world in judging prose is often undecided as to what is literature and what is not. We are all agreed that we cannot include in literature every form of written or printed matter. But where does literature begin or end? Must we exclude almost all science, much history, most fiction? On one or two points at least the Greeks never wavered. When the early glamour —the sense of mystery and almost of magic

—attaching to the discovery of writing had passed away, writing was at first thought of chiefly as a mechanical aid to memory. It saved from oblivion the inspirations of the Muse. Outside poetry its early uses were of the practical kind : it was employed for registering treaties and contracts and for keeping accounts.[1] So far, however, as it was designed to serve purely material ends, it formed part of the prosaic order of life and lacked the dignity of art. In order to enter into the domain of art, in order to become literature,

---

[1] Euripides notes accurately the early use of writing for practical purposes—letters or messages, wills, contracts, etc. ; see Fr. (Palamedes) 578 Nauck :

> τὰ τῆς γε λήθης φάρμακ' ὀρθώσας μόνος
> ἄφωνα φωνήεντα συλλαβὰς τιθεὶς
> ἐξηῦρον ἀνθρώποισι γράμματ' εἰδέναι,
> ὥστ' οὐ παρόντα ποντίας ὑπὲρ πλακὸς
> τἀκεῖ κατ' οἴκους πάντ' ἐπίστασθαι καλῶς,
> παισίν τε τὸν θνήσκοντα χρημάτων μέτρον
> γράψαντας εἰπεῖν, τὸν λαβόντα δ' εἰδέναι.
> ἃ δ' εἰς ἔριν πίπτουσιν ἄνθρωποι πέρι,
> δέλτος διαιρεῖ, κοὐκ ἐᾷ ψευδῆ λέγειν.

Cp. schol. on *Odyss.* viii. 163 ὅθεν καὶ τοὺς Φοίνικας ἐμπόρους ὑπὸ τῆς χρείας αὐτῆς ('purely practical needs') ἐπὶ τὴν τῶν γραμμάτων εὕρεσιν ἐλθεῖν.

the written word must needs invest itself with a new character. First, it must become an expression of human thought or emotion. The bare cold fact must pass through a human medium ; it must take the personality of the writer, or be coloured by the collective experience of the race. Secondly, some beauty of form must be impressed upon it—a beauty that should be tested by the ear as well as by the mind.

These principles had long been instinctively recognised in poetry. As soon as Greek reflection applied itself to the difficult problem of how to write prose, the conviction slowly took shape, that if prose is to be more than a lifeless record of facts and figures ; if it is to exert its full force in civic life as an instrument of persuasion ; if it is to be of enduring value as a vehicle of discovered truth, it must, like verse, submit itself to the law of beauty. Style is no mere concession to human infirmity ; it is the imperious demand of art ; and through art alone can the perishable word clothe itself in lasting form. Even the scientific writers of

Greece sought to stamp the impress of art, some grace of style, upon works which otherwise could not, they felt, pass outside the narrow circle of specialists. The great treatise of Hippocrates on medicine begins with the words : ' Life is short : Art is long : Opportunity fleeting : Experiment hazardous : Judgment difficult.' [1] At once you hear the tones of one who is an artist in prose ; this, you say, is literature as well as science. With what delighted surprise we should to-day greet a medical treatise with such an opening !

In our own day the style of prose is subjected to two different and even opposing influences. On the one hand, those who feel the need of making prose artistic, easily become artificial : they rely on the suggestive more than on the expressive force of words ; they adopt a manner of writing which is far-fetched, allusive, recondite. Those, on the other hand, who feel the need of making prose practical, of producing an effect strong and immediate,

---

[1] Hippocr. *Aphor.* i. 1 ὁ βίος βραχύς, ἡ δὲ τέχνη μακρή, ὁ δὲ καιρὸς ὀξύς, ἡ δὲ πεῖρα σφαλερή, ἡ δὲ κρίσις χαλεπή.

fall into exaggeration in the desire to be emphatic. In either case the language is strained. Style becomes in the one instance affected ; in the other, breathless and in a hurry. But the great prose writers move us by their powerful simplicity, their quiet strength, their sense of measure and proportion, even by what has been called their ' grand leisureliness ' of manner. They recall the Eastern proverb, ' Hurry comes of the devil, slowness of God.'

No more wholesome corrective of any false ideals of prose writing can be found than the study of Attic prose masterpieces. At first perhaps they strike us as cold. The rhetorical manner, the pomp of phrase of aristocratic Rome, is more congenial to modern taste. We are accustomed to sonorous periphrases, to pathetic and emotional appeals, to saying rather more than we mean, in the hope that people may be convinced that we mean something. But by degrees we become conscious not only of the charm, but also of the power of simplicity. We see that an exaggerated phrase is often due to mere ignorance of

the 'proper' word.   Monotonous splendour
soon wearies us, and we confess the truth of
Aristotle's remark, that 'a too brilliant diction obscures the expression of character and
thought.' [1]

The Athenians disliked phrase-making.
Overdone ornament did not, in their judgment,
adorn but deface.   The beauty of prose was
felt to lie in the texture of the whole, rather
than in isolated phrases or passages.   To present an idea in its true proportions, the parts
being skilfully adjusted to one another, and
the proper values of each given by contrast and
arrangement—this was their chief concern.   It
would, of course, be misleading to speak of
Attic authors as if they all wrote in one style.
The broad contrasts between them are numerous and striking ; the finer shades of difference
are endlessly various.   But there are certain
common characteristics which mark the Attic
manner.   The speech is that of daily life, direct
and lucid ; of men who are accustomed to easy

---

[1] *Poet.* xxiv. 11. 1460 b 4 ἀποκρύπτει γὰρ πάλιν ἡ λίαν
λαμπρὰ λέξις τά τε ἤθη καὶ τὰς διανοίας.

human intercourse without artificial barrier or restraint, who desire to understand, and to be understood of others. But the colloquial idiom is raised above the commonplace. It has an added touch of distinction, unobtrusive but unmistakable ; a beauty or charm which conceals the hand of the artist ; sometimes, too, an energy, a compactness of phrase—quite unlike the flowing grace of the Ionian writers—which reminds us, perhaps too forcibly, that this finely tempered instrument of language has been forged or sharpened in the rhetorical schools.

It is a style scrupulous in the purity of its diction, in avoidance of provincialisms, in the effort to hit the right, rather than the approximately right word. It has a certain well-bred elegance, which cannot be mistaken for pedantry. It obeys, moreover, the law of reserve : it wins the goodwill of the reader by leaving something to his own intelligence.[1] In the

---

[1] Cp. Theophrastus ap. Demetr. *De Eloc.* 222 οὐ πάντα ἐπ' ἀκριβείας δεῖ μακρηγορεῖν, ἀλλ' ἔνια καταλιπεῖν καὶ τῷ ἀκροατῇ συνιέναι καὶ λογίζεσθαι ἐξ αὑτοῦ· συνεὶς γὰρ τὸ ἐλλειφθὲν ὑπὸ σοῦ οὐκ ἀκροατὴς μόνον, ἀλλὰ καὶ μάρτυς σου γίνεται, καὶ ἅμα εὐμενέστερος.

Q

region of feeling it is discreet and guarded. It refuses to speak in accents of emotion where emotion is wanting ; but where real passion has to be expressed, the glow of feeling is at once revealed in the rising tone and in rhythms in which we seem to overhear the very vibrations of the voice. Still, even in its impassioned and imaginative modes of utterance Attic prose retains the sense of measure, the precision, the sobriety, which constitute its essential character. It is just this union of passion and self-restraint, the appeal to the reason no less than to the emotions, that lends to Greek oratory its incomparable force.

There was a moment in the fifth century B.C. when the Athenians, shaping their prose under the influence of the Sophists, were tempted to take up the cult of ' Art for Art's sake,' and to aim at æsthetic expression apart from the meaning to be conveyed. They would hardly indeed have subscribed to Flaubert's saying, that ' a beautiful verse meaning nothing is superior to a less beautiful verse meaning something ' : still it was in that direc-

tion that the danger lay even in prose composition.   But the just literary instinct of the
people, combined with their practical sagacity
and the vigour of their political life, saved them
from this alluring evil.   That the expression
in words should be exactly adequate to the
thought,[1] and should also charm the ear,
became the guiding principle of their literary
art.   The dislike of the Athenians for false
ornament, their intolerance of exaggeration,
their power of direct vision, led them to find
the perfection of language in keeping closer
than any other people to what was simple
and natural.   Thus they found it possible to
reconcile their disdain of mere phrase-making
with an exquisite delight in beautiful and
harmonious words.

The value attached to literary form by all
antiquity, Greek and Roman, is, as stated in
general terms, a familiar and trite idea.   But
it is of capital importance to remember that
in testing beauty of form the Greeks submitted

---

[1] Cp. Lysias ap. Greg. Cor. p. 4 ἡ γὰρ γλῶττα νοῦν οὔτε πολὺν
οὔτε μικρὸν ἔχει, ὁ δὲ νοῦς, ᾧ μὲν πολύ, πολύς, ᾧ δὲ μικρόν, μικρός.

the written word, prose and verse alike, to the
immediate judgment of the ear. The language in which the later Greek critics speak
of the harmonies of prose composition might,
by a modern reader, be suspected of some
unreality. But the truth is that the power
of sound, the rhythm and music of the spoken
word, was felt by the Greeks in a degree we
cannot readily comprehend. 'With harmonious
arrangement of words comes Literature in its
many kinds.'[1] 'There is a marvellous attraction and enthralling charm in appropriate and
striking words. . . . Beautiful words are the
very and peculiar light of the mind.'[2] The
Chinese, whose language like that of the
Greeks is distinguished by the musical, as
opposed to the stress, accent, are said to be
the only modern people who are equally
sensitive to the æsthetic sound of words.

---

[1] Dionys. Hal. *De Comp. Verb.* c. xvi παρὰ δὲ τὰς τῶν
ὀνομάτων ἁρμονίας πολύμορφος ὁ λόγος γίνεται (Trans. Saintsbury, *Loci Critici*, p. 34).

[2] Longinus *De Subl.* c. xxx. 1 ἡ τῶν κυρίων καὶ μεγαλοπρεπῶν
ὀνομάτων ἐκλογὴ θαυμαστῶς ἄγει καὶ κατακηλεῖ τοὺς ἀκούοντας.
. . . φῶς γὰρ τῷ ὄντι ἴδιον τοῦ νοῦ τὰ καλὰ ὀνόματα.

The art of printing has done much to
dull our literary perceptions. Words have a
double virtue—that which resides in the sense
and that which resides in the sound. We
miss much of the charm if the eye is made
to do duty also for the ear. The words, bereft
of their vocal force, are but half alive on the
printed page. The music of verse, when repeated only to the inward ear, comes as a faint
echo. But it is perhaps in prose that we
have most to learn from the ancients in respect
of style. They observed the movements of
prose rhythm, they felt its harmonies, the
happy union of music and meaning, the adjustment of sounds to the mood or feeling they
would convey—all this in a manner impossible
save to those with whom eye and ear, soul
and sense, have been trained to work together
in perfect correspondence. It is a fact but
little known that throughout the Greek period,
and far into the days of the Roman empire—
to the third and fourth century of our era—
the custom survived of reading both prose and
verse, not silently, but aloud and in company.

There is a curious passage in Augustine's *Con-fessions*, one of the few in ancient literature where silent reading is mentioned.[1]   He there tells of the difficulty he had in getting access to his master Ambrose, whose rare hours of leisure were spent in reading, and who was one day observed to run his eye silently over the page, while 'his voice and tongue were still.'   Various reasons are then suggested to account for so strange a departure from the common practice.

'To write and read comes by nature,' said Dogberry.   Epicurus, it seems, held a like opinion : 'there is no difficulty,' he said, 'in writing.'[2]   The Greeks on the whole did not find it so.   Verse came to them almost as their native speech.   From their cradle they had the gift of song.   But the language of prose was built up by long and laborious

[1] August. *Confess.* vi. 3 'cum legebat oculi ducebantur per paginas, et cor intellectum rimabatur, vox autem et lingua quiescebant.'   In the Classical age ἀναγιγνώσκειν is rarely used of silent reading, the full phrase being ἀναγιγνώσκειν πρὸς ἑαυτόν.

[2] Dionys. Hal. *De Comp. Verb.* c. xxiv.

discipline. Those who first wrote prose had to create it; they had no foreign models, no tradition to guide them. The only tradition was the tradition of poetry.[1] From this, by degrees, they strove to set themselves free. But they were haunted by Epic reminiscences, by the old poetic diction, by the rhythm and roll of the hexameter. Even in the philosopher Heraclitus hexameter endings are not uncommon;[2] and in Herodotus we find a greater number of beginnings and endings of hexameter lines than in any later author. These early writers easily slip into metre, especially when the thought and diction become elevated; just as blank verse is always forcing its way into English prose. In Greece snatches of metre and other poetical ornaments were at first sought out as an embellishment of prose. In time the practice was

---

[1] Cp. Strabo i. 2. 16 πρώτιστα γὰρ ἡ ποιητικὴ κατασκευὴ παρῆλθεν εἰς τὸ μέσον καὶ εὐδοκίμησεν· εἶτα ἐκείνην μιμούμενοι, λύσαντες τὸ μέτρον, τἆλλα δὲ φυλάξαντες τὰ ποιητικά, συνέγραψαν οἱ περὶ Κάδμον καὶ Φερεκύδη καὶ Ἑκαταῖον.

[2] *E.g.* μαρτυρέει παρεόντας ἀπεῖναι—τὸ μὲν ἥμισυ γῆ, τὸ δὲ ἥμισυ πρηστήρ.

decisively condemned by all good critics.
Aristotle, who laid it down that the styles of
poetry and prose are distinct,[1] also insisted that
'prose should have rhythm but not metre, or
it will be a poem : the rhythm, however, must
not be over-exact ; it must be kept within due
limits.'[2] What the due limits were, was a
question variously answered. For the rest, the
rule that prose should be rhythmical, became
an accepted canon of criticism. Plato goes
so far as to discover a moral danger in prose
compositions which lack rhythm or harmony ;
to his mind they indicate some disorder within
the soul.[3]

While prose rhythm was not only permitted but enjoined, another and cognate
question, that of poetic prose, was more open
to debate. Literary taste was at first divided
on the point. When literature descended from

---

[1] *Rhet.* iii. 1. 9. 1404 a 28 ἑτέρα λόγου καὶ ποιήσεως λέξις
ἐστίν.

[2] *Ib.* iii. 8. 3. 1408 b 30 διὸ ῥυθμὸν δεῖ ἔχειν τὸν λόγον,
μέτρον δὲ μή, ποίημα γὰρ ἔσται. ῥυθμὸν δὲ μὴ ἀκριβῶς. τοῦτο
δὲ ἔσται ἐὰν μέχρι του ᾖ. See also an instructive passage
De Subl. c. xli.   [3] *Laws* vii. 810 B.

her chariot of poetry—to use the metaphor so
frequently employed by Greek writers [1]—she
affected the manner of 'high-stepping' prose
rather than resign herself at once to 'march
on foot' (πεζὸς λόγος). Gorgias (fifth century
B.C.) was one of the first to invoke these graces
of poetry.[2] Yet he and his school worked
at the language in the spirit of artists ; and,
though their zeal betrayed them into some
overwrought ingenuity, an excessive use of
figures, wearisome antithesis, verbal assonances,
and so forth, still they had a true presenti-
ment of the capacities of Greek speech. They
felt that it was possible to impart to prose
a nobility of its own ; that it could be lifted
above the idiom of daily life, and yet acquire
force and precision. 'It is the perfection of
style,' says Aristotle, 'to be clear without being
mean ' ; [3]—but, he proceeds, 'by deviating sometimes from the normal idiom,' 'by adding some

---

[1] *E.g.* Plut. *De Pyth. Orac.* 24 κατέβη μὲν ἀπὸ τῶν μέτρων
ὥσπερ ὀχημάτων ἡ ἱστορία.

[2] See Jebb *Att. Or.* i. cxxiii. ff.

[3] *Poet.* xxii. 1. 1456 a 18 λέξεως δὲ ἀρετὴ σαφῆ καὶ μὴ
ταπεινὴν εἶναι.

element of novelty or surprise,' 'the language
will gain distinction' (τὸ μὴ ἰδιωτικόν).[1]   In
his judgment, however, Gorgias exceeded the
proper limits of such deviation.   His prose approached too nearly to the poetical manner,
and on this account he is censured more than
once in the *Rhetoric*.[2]

It so happens that a few specimens are
elsewhere also preserved of Gorgias' metaphorical and poetical style.   'At last Sleep
begins to lay me beside his brother Death'—
is one of his sayings in extreme old age:[3]
another is : 'I take my departure as from a
lodging ruinous and decayed.'[4]   As isolated
sayings, these could hardly offend Greek, any
more than they do English taste.   But in
both languages they belong rather to the order

---

[1] *Poet.* xxii. 4. 1458 b 2 ff.

[2] *Rhet.* iii. 1. 9. 1404 a 25 ff. ποιητικὴ πρώτη ἐγένετο λέξις,
οἷον ἡ Γοργίου, καὶ νῦν ἔτι οἱ πολλοὶ τῶν ἀπαιδεύτων τοὺς
τοιούτους οἴονται διαλέγεσθαι κάλλιστα. τοῦτο δ' οὐκ ἔστιν,
κ.τ.λ. *Ib.* iii. 3. 4. 1406 b 9 ff.

[3] Aelian *V. H.* ii. 35 ἤδη με ὁ ὕπνος ἄρχεται παρακατα-
τίθεσθαι τἀδελφῷ.

[4] Arsenius *Praeclara Dicta Philosophorum* ὥσπερ ἐκ σαπροῦ
καὶ ῥέοντος συνοικίου ἀσμένως ἀπαλλάττομαι.

of poetry, and could not appropriately be used
in prose except at rare moments.   Of the
metaphors which Aristotle cites and censures in
prose, two, perhaps, deserve mention.   One is
from the pen of Gorgias : ' You sowed in shame,
to reap in ruin.'   ' Too grand and tragic,' says
Aristotle ; [1] and familiar as is the metaphor of
sowing and reaping, I think we should concur
with him.   Even to modern ears the saying is
high-flown in so antithetic a form, and it would
need a very impassioned context to justify it.
It is otherwise with the metaphor he quotes
with disapproval from Alcidamas (one of the
school of Gorgias) describing the *Odyssey* as ' a
fair mirror of human life.' [2]   The most fastidious
modern critic would not carp at this.   But the
word κάτοπτρον in its metaphorical sense must
have had something far more daring and
unaccustomed for a Greek than the word
' mirror ' has in English.   Aristotle's censure
of the same writer for employing ornamental

---

[1] *Rhet.* iii. 3. 4. 1406 b 9 σὺ δὲ ταῦτα αἰσχρῶς μὲν ἔσπειρας,
κακῶς δὲ ἐθέρισας.

[2] *Ib.* iii. 3. 4. 1406 b 12 καλὸν ἀνθρωπίνου βίου κάτοπτρον.

epithets 'not as the sauce of the discourse but as the dish,'[1] is levelled at a fault of taste into which the Greeks seldom fell.

Aristotle does not appear to have appreciated either the suggestive capacity of words or their musical value. The most instructive commentary on the emotional power of sound, as it was felt by the Greeks even in prose literature, is to be found in Dionysius of Halicarnassus, a critic and grammarian who lived at Rome in the Augustan age.[2] Many of his literary judgments are prejudiced and unprofitable, but of his fine perception of the harmonies of Greek speech we can entertain no reasonable doubt. In an essay entitled *On the Arrangement of Words*, that is little read even by scholars, he assumes that the ear demands nobility and charm in literary expression as truly as the eye does in a picture or a statue (c. x.). He holds that the magic of style depends less on the apt choice

---

[1] *Rhet.* iii. 3. 3. 1406 a 18 οὐ γὰρ ἡδύσματι χρῆται ἀλλ' ὡς ἐδέσματι τοῖς ἐπιθέτοις.

[2] On Dionysius as a literary critic see the valuable edition of *The Three Literary Essays* by W. Rhys Roberts (Cambridge Press 1901), pp. 1-49.

(ἐκλογή) of words than on the manner in which they are disposed (σύνθεσις) within the sentence. Alter their arrangement and you destroy the total effect : for arrangement is like the Homeric Athene, who can at will make Odysseus mendicant or warrior, mean or mighty (c. ii.-iv.). Taking the alphabet itself he examines the letters from the euphonic point of view (c. xiv.). Phonetics, it may be observed, never with the Greeks became an independent science. The inquiries made into the physiology of sound had all a bearing on the study of rhetoric, the object being simply to discover what sounds were beautiful or the reverse. Hence the link was a close one which united phonetics on the one hand with metric and music on the other ; and it lay within the domain of the musician rather than of the grammarian to classify the letters of the alphabet. True to this principle Dionysius, in estimating the elemental sounds, relies on the authority of Aristoxenus, the author of the famous treatise on music. He arranges the vowels in order of euphonic value : α, η, ω, υ, ι. Among the consonants, sigma is a letter 'without grace or sweetness, and if too frequently employed becomes very painful. The sibilant sound seems characteristic of the voice of the brute rather than of rational man.'[1] Some poets, he adds, composed whole odes without a sigma;[2] and elsewhere we read of a *tour de force* of the kind attributed to Pindar.[3]

We cannot here follow Dionysius in his intricate distinctions of style. I would refer only to a single chapter in which he appears as the hierophant of a hidden art, one who is prepared to initiate us into the innermost secret of literature. He asks the question *How a prose work may resemble a beautiful poem.* The phrases with which he prefaces the inquiry are borrowed from the mysteries of Eleusis :

'These things indeed are of the nature of mysteries and not to be divulged to the vulgar.

---

[1] Dionys. Hal. *De Comp. Verb.* c. xiv. ἄχαρι δὲ καὶ ἀηδὲς τὸ σ, καὶ εἰ πλεονάσειε σφόδρα λυπεῖ· θηριώδους γὰρ καὶ ἀλόγου μᾶλλον ἢ λογικῆς ἐφάπτεσθαι δοκεῖ φωνῆς ὁ συριγμός.

[2] εἰσὶ δὲ οἱ ἀσίγμους ᾠδὰς ὅλας ἐποίουν.

[3] Athen. x. 455 C.

It would, therefore, be no impertinence should I invite only the privileged few to be present at the holy rites of literature, and bid the profane close the gates of their ears. For some there are who in sheer ignorance make a mockery of things most serious.' [1]

He then expounds the doctrine of rhythmical prose, working on the text supplied by Aristotle's *Rhetoric.* Prose must be rhythmical but not metrical, poetical without being a poem, and melodious without being a lyric. Next he selects passages from Demosthenes, which he submits to a searching and minute analysis on the side of rhythm. Some of his distinctions, it must be owned, bear traces of the over-elaboration of the rhetorical schools. But we cannot dismiss his general criticism as unsound or fanciful. The whole history of the evolution of Greek prose, and the practice of the great

---

[1] Dionys. Hal. *De Comp. Verb.* c. xxv μυστηρίοις μὲν οὖν ἔοικεν ἤδη ταῦτα, καὶ οὐκ εἰς πολλοὺς οἷά τέ ἐστιν ἐκφέρεσθαι. ὥστ' οὐκ ἂν εἴην φορτικός, εἰ παρακαλοίην, οἷς θέμις ἐστίν, ἥκειν ἐπὶ τὰς τελετὰς τοῦ λόγου, θύρας δ' ἐπίθεσθαι λέγοιμι ταῖς ἀκοαῖς τοὺς βεβήλους. εἰς γέλωτα γὰρ ἔνιοι λαμβάνουσι τὰ σπουδαιότατα δι' ἀπειρίαν.

masters of the art, support his main contention. The trained oratorical ear was acutely sensitive to euphonious combinations of sounds. No pains were spared that words might be linked together by easy and continuous articulation. Rough and clashing syllables were avoided, and even two vowels in consecutive words were seldom allowed to collide. We can trace, moreover, the stages by which the ample movement of the oratorical period was developed—how the clauses that follow one another in logical sequence and subordination, come to be linked together in a larger rhythmical structure. Recent critics following in the steps of Dionysius have attempted to define more accurately the rules of rhythm and harmony which govern the prose of Demosthenes. But such analysis, probably, can never be more than partially successful. The Demosthenic rhythm in its infinite variety refuses to adjust itself to any rigid framework. No one can fail to catch something of its manifold movement, its great rise and fall ; but its laws are as free as the emotion to which it responds. In

vain we seek an exact rhythmic correspondence
between the members of a period or of successive periods. Rhythmic symmetry of a kind
there surely is ; but the attempt to follow it out
in minor details succeeds, too often, only by
cutting up the period into artificial sections,
without due regard to oral delivery or to the
natural pauses of the voice.

The modern world has grown dull to the
cadences of prose. We read of Greek and
Roman audiences being painfully affected by
inharmonious combinations of sound. There
is probably no conceivable dissonance which
would cause neuralgia to the unfastidious ears
of a British audience. English is itself in truth
a most difficult language to render musical. It
is only when we venture to write it ourselves
that we become aware how ugly it can be
made, and wonder at the full harmonies that
can be drawn out by one who knows all the
tones of the instrument.

Now and then, by a rare chance, we are
admitted to the confidence of a writer who
has mastered the art. There is an article by

R

R. L. Stevenson on ' Style in Literature,'[1] which
is a pretty precise modern parallel to the speculations of Dionysius.   Stevenson, we may be
sure, had never read Dionysius—probably had
never heard of him.   But his manner of treatment is curiously similar.   ' Each phrase in
literature,' says Stevenson, ' is built of sounds,
as each phrase in music consists of notes.   One
sound suggests, echoes, demands and harmonizes
with another ; and the art of rightly using these
concordances is the final art in literature.'[2]   In
bad writers ' you will find cacophony supreme,
the rattle of incongruous consonants only
relieved by the jaw-breaking hiatus, and whole
phrases not to be articulated by the powers
of man.'   ' You may follow the adventures of
a letter through any passage that has particularly pleased you ; find it, perhaps, denied
awhile to tantalize the ear ; find it fired again
at you in a whole broadside ; or find it pass

---

[1] *Contemp. Rev.* 1885.

[2] Cp. Dionys. Hal. *De Comp. Verb.* c. xvi ὥστε πολλὴ
ἀνάγκη καλὴν μὲν εἶναι λέξιν ἐν ᾗ καλά ἐστιν ὀνόματα, καλῶν
δὲ ὀνομάτων συλλαβάς τε καὶ γράμματα καλὰ αἴτια εἶναι, ἡδεῖάν
τε διάλεκτον ἐκ τῶν ἡδυνόντων τὴν ἀκοὴν γίνεσθαι.

into congenerous sounds, one liquid or labial
melting away into another.'   Instances he then
gives from Milton's prose, from Shakespeare
and Coleridge, tracking in each case the recur-
ring letters.   And as to the rhythm, he writes :
' Each phrase of each sentence, like an air or
recitative in music, should be so artfully com-
pounded out of longs and shorts, out of accented
and unaccented syllables, as to gratify the
sensual ear.   And of this the ear is the sole
judge.'   He ends a long inquiry by observing :
' We begin to see now what an intricate affair
is any perfect passage ; how many faculties,
whether of taste or pure reason, must be held
upon the stretch to make it ; and why when it
is made, it should afford so complete a pleasure.
. . . We need not wonder then if perfect
sentences are rare, and perfect pages rarer.'

Fascinating, however, as are such disclosures
of the inner mechanism of the craft, may we
not feel confident that the method of production
is one thing, and the method of analysis
another ; and that neither Demosthenes nor
Milton—nor Stevenson himself at his best—

were solicitous to count their longs and shorts, or consciously played the game of hide-and-seek with the letters ?

Let us now pass to the age of the Antonines —the second century of our era—and glance at the work of the one man of literary genius whom that age produced : an original writer, who had also many of the gifts of a great critic—Lucian, the Syrian, of Samosata. A pamphleteer by instinct, a light and airy spirit with an exuberant and poetic fancy, a sparkling irony, a singular freshness and delicacy of tone —of all his gifts his inimitable ease and naturalness of manner was perhaps the chief secret of his art. He had a native dislike for falsehood and insincerity in literature as in life. In an age of tasteless pedantry he stood out as a model of simplicity and unaffected good taste. The literary artists of the day— ' Sophists ' as they were called—were as a rule itinerant rhetoricians, whose business it was to handle any theme effectively at short notice, and execute variations upon it in brilliant and acrobatic manner. They had a pretty knack of turning phrases ; but their ingenious conceits concealed an inner unreality and poverty of thought. Lucian set his face against the pretentiousness, the affectation, the hollow imposture which passed for art. His own literary criticism is occasional and unsystematic, conveyed for the most part in parody or lightly veiled irony ; but none the less it is original and genuine criticism.

In the pamphlet entitled *The Teacher of Orators* he lays down certain rules which may be thus summarised : First, bring to your subject ignorance and audacity, a stentorian voice, an exquisite toilette, and some fifteen or twenty old Attic words, which must be freely sprinkled as a garnishing to your discourse. They are always beautiful, even when they are nothing to the purpose.[1] Next, press forward, speak fluently, do not pause to think. Do not trouble to put things in their proper order. Thirdly— and above all—have a chorus of friends to

---

[1] *Rhet. Praec.* § 16 καθάπερ τι ἥδυσμα ἐπίταττε αὐτῶν. § 18 καὶ ἐπίπαστα τὰ ὀλίγα ἐκεῖνα ὀνόματα ἐπιπολαζέτω καὶ ἐπανθείτω· . . . καλὰ γάρ ἐστι καὶ εἰκῇ λεγόμενα.

applaud you.   We observe here the allusion to
old Attic words.   The love of archaic phrases,
which had been one of the passing affectations
of early prose, has now reappeared.   Words
were unearthed or 'dug up,'[1] no one knew
whence, by persons who had never read the
ancient writers, and who opened none but the
newest books.   The taste for archaisms and
the craze for novelty generally go together in
decadent minds.[2]   In another satire, the *Lexi-
phanes*, Lucian administers a drastic medical
treatment to a patient suffering from this
fantastic disorder ; and finally dismisses him
with a little homily on literary education,
which has in it the ring of real conviction.
The closing words (§§ 23-24) are to this effect :
'Give up the quest for outlandish phrases ;
think first of the sense, then of the words.

---

[1] *Lexiph.* § 16 τοσοῦτον ἑσμὸν ἀτόπων καὶ διαστρόφων
ὀνομάτων, ὧν τὰ μὲν αὐτὸς ἐποίησας, τὰ δὲ κατορωρυγμένα
ποθὲν ἀνασπῶν κ.τ.λ.

[2] Cp. *De Subl.* c. v. τὸ περὶ τὰς νοήσεις καινόσπουδον, περὶ
ὃ δὴ μάλιστα κορυβαντιῶσιν οἱ νῦν, ' that quest after novelty in
thought which leads our folk of to-day so mad a dance ' (Saintsbury, *Loci Critici*, p. 42).

Follow the ancient models instead of moulding yourself on the poorest productions of the latest sophist. Be not beguiled by the wind-flowers of speech (αἱ ἀνεμῶναι τῶν λόγων), but nourish your literary sense on the fortifying food of athletes.'

In Lucian's literary criticisms there is always a tacit reference to the great traditions of the past. One of the evils he discerned was that the various forms of literature were encroaching each on another's sphere ; natural boundaries were being effaced and there was a confusion of kinds. The pervading influence of rhetoric more than any other single cause brought about this anarchy of taste. Rhetoric was the one educational discipline of the Roman empire and the passport to success in every walk of life. Indeed we find the word 'eloquentia' employed by Roman writers as the comprehensive term for every form of literary composition, grave and gay, prose and verse. Poetry slowly withered as rhetoric gained ground ; and even literary critics in turn came to treat poetry from the point of

view of the rhetorical schools, till the question
was seriously raised by a Roman writer,
Annaeus Florus, of the second century A.D.,
whether Virgil was an orator or a poet.

Of all kinds of prose composition history
suffered most from this subtle form of corruption.   It was held to be a province of
rhetoric ; its special department was that of
panegyric.[1]   The subject to be chosen must be
one that was flattering to national vanity and
that admitted of skilful embellishment.   The
art of rhetorical amplification would find full
scope in the fictitious speeches which had
become a fixed tradition in historical writing.
But history was at the same time menaced by
the inroad of poetry.[2]   It was the business of
poetry to supply the engaging falsehood, to
adorn the legends, to give an imaginative
colouring to the digressions, and offer to the
weary traveller pleasant resting-places by the

---

[1] Cp. Hermog. *De Ideis* p. 417. 28 πάντως δεῖ καὶ τοὺς
ἱστοριογράφους ἐν τοῖς πανηγυρικοῖς τετάχθαι.

[2] Lucian *De Hist. Conscr.* § 8 ἀγνοεῖν ἐοίκασιν οἱ τοιοῦτοι
ὡς ποιητικῆς μὲν καὶ ποιημάτων ἄλλαι ὑποσχέσεις καὶ κανόνες
ἴδιοι, ἱστορίας δὲ ἄλλοι.

way. Thus the danger which the Greeks
surmounted in their vigorous prime, when prose
began to advance along the lines of poetry,
now, in a new form, assailed historical writers,
both Greek and Roman.

In his pamphlet *How to write History*
Lucian puts in a plea for accuracy and
sobriety ; he protests—as also did Polybius—
against turning history into panegyric.[1] He
ridicules the writers who affect a vulgarly
picturesque style or one overloaded with
descriptive detail (§§ 19-20). No less does
he condemn that jumble of styles in which
fine writing is interspersed with touches of
slang—'the buskin of tragedy on one foot,
and a slipper on the other.'[2] He disallows
the lawless poetic fancy by which history
becomes 'a sort of prosaic poetry.'[3] His own

[1] *De Hist. Conscr.* § 7 ('a great gulf is fixed' between history
and panegyric) : ἀγνοοῦντες ὡς οὐ στενῷ τῷ ἰσθμῷ διώρισται
καὶ διατετείχισται ἡ ἱστορία πρὸς τὸ ἐγκώμιον.

[2] *Ib.* § 22 ὥστε τὸ πρᾶγμα ἐοικὸς εἶναι τραγῳδῷ, τὸν ἕτερον
μὲν πόδα ἐπ' ἐμβάτου ὑψηλοῦ ἐπιβεβηκότι, θατέρῳ δὲ σάνδαλον
ὑποδεδεμένῳ.

[3] *Ib.* § 8 ἡ ἱστορία δέ, ἤν τινα κολακείαν τοιαύτην προσλάβῃ,
τί ἄλλο ἢ πέζῃ τις ποιητικὴ γίγνεται ;

conception of what a historian ought to be is
in marked contrast with the character of the
historian of the day—his servility, his disregard
of truth, his straining after dramatic effect.
The historian should be 'a free man, fearless,
incorruptible, the friend of truth,' 'owning no
country, no sovereign, no king';[1] one who
writes not for the praise of the hour but for
all time to come.[2]

The triple alliance of history, poetry, and
rhetoric injuriously affected, through the course
of centuries, the historical tradition of Europe.
In recent years a sharp reaction has set in
against what is called the literary influence in
history. The Muse of history is exhorted to
cast aside her literary trappings and assume her
severest aspect. She must make herself
scientific. Under the æsthetic influence, Seeley
urges, history becomes pictorial; the pictorial
point of view is apt to overshadow the historical;

[1] *De Hist. Conscr.* § 41 ἄφοβος, ἀδέκαστος, ἐλεύθερος, παρ-
ρησίας καὶ ἀληθείας φίλος, . . . ἴσος δικαστὴς εὔνους ἅπασιν,
. . . ξένος ἐν τοῖς βιβλίοις, καὶ ἄπολις, αὐτόνομος, ἀβασίλευτος.

[2] *Ib.* § 61 μὴ πρὸς τὸ παρὸν μόνον ὁρῶν γράφε, . . . ἀλλὰ
τοῦ σύμπαντος αἰῶνος ἐστοχασμένος.

a biographical interest is substituted for a
political. Attention is concentrated on the
mere externals of an event, on its scenic
accessories, on all that is personal and dramatic
and that invites literary handling. Whereas
many of the most important events are con-
fessedly dull reading, great political changes
being brought about without pomp or glitter,
the literary estimate falsifies the true proportions of things. The artistic historian rejects
elements of serious interest in order to satisfy
the taste for the picturesque.

Few will deny the solid truth that underlies
this criticism. But we cannot lightly accept
the suggestion that history should emancipate
herself from literature. Seeley himself fortunately possessed so fine a literary gift as to be
unable to carry out his own theory. But the
summons has again been addressed to history
—and in a more peremptory form—by the
present holder of the chair at Cambridge, to
quit her old associates and come out into a
place of freedom.[1] In the view of this dis-

[1] *Inaugural Lecture*, J. B. Bury, Cambridge Press, 1903.

tinguished writer history is not, as for Seeley, limited to the mass of facts which form the material of political science. It embraces other groups of facts and is more comprehensive in its scope. Still for him too history is a science not an art ; 'a science no less and no more ' ; in close relation with 'the sciences which deal objectively with the facts of the universe.' 'To clothe the story of a human society in a literary dress is no more the part of a historian as a historian, than it is the part of an astronomer as an astronomer to present in an artistic shape the story of the stars.'

Yet may we not urge that the form of a work must be mainly determined by the nature of the subject-matter ? Human action cannot be told in just the terms applicable to cosmic processes. History is not merely the story of movements, of institutions, or of changes in the order of society. It is also the story of men, doing, feeling, thinking ; acting as individuals, though within and in relation to the political organism. A purely scientific history could hardly touch the fringe of the inward world of human motive and human personality. That world, with its reactions on the outer, can never be reduced to the certitude of scientific truth : its facts cannot be tested or authenticated by the methods which strict science recognises. They need some divining power, some faculty of imaginative interpretation to make them intelligible ; and such a faculty demands the art of literary expression. Different periods, again, call for different kinds of writing. In describing scenes of stirring and dramatic interest it is right that the style should reflect the colour and movement of the time. Great deeds should be nobly told. There are other periods which carry within them the silent growth of institutions or the shaping of events still in the future. It is the part of the literary historian not to omit these less inspiring pages of history, but to relate them in a manner adapted to the subject. We are here within the proper region of literature.

'What a pity it is,' says Edward FitzGerald, 'that only Lying Histories are readable.' Would

not, however, the unreadable histories—divorced
from the literary art and omitting many vital
but non-scientific facts—be also to a large
extent untrue ?　History, in short, would seem
to be partly a science, and partly an art.　It
is a very human affair, this story of the past,
and it must be so told that men will read it
with sympathy and even with delight.　Let
us search the records, collate the manuscripts,
investigate the sources, classify and collect the
facts : yet all this is not yet history, but the
materials of history—' not tragedy,' in Plato's
phrase, ' but the preliminaries of tragedy.' [1]　It
remains for the writer of genius and imagination
to fuse the elements, the outward and the
inward facts, into an orderly whole.　The
antithesis between history and literary history
is surely a false one.　History rightly told is
literature ; but it is not therefore rhetorical,
unreal, fantastic.　We do not ask the historian
to be ' the epic poet or ballad writer in verse.' [2]
We do say that he should be at once a literary

---

[1] Plat. *Phaedr.* 269 A τὰ πρὸ τραγῳδίας ἀλλ' οὐ τὰ τραγικά.
[2] Seeley, *Introduction to Political Science*, p. 27.

man and a man of science.   The task of writing
literary history becomes indeed every day
more difficult owing to specialised learning,
the accumulation of materials, and the stricter
standard of truth.   To be a literary historian
will probably be a rare achievement in the
future.   But the ideal should not on that
account be lowered.   What is needed is, not
that history should cease to be literary, but
that it should be literary in a higher than the
ordinary sense ; the style should be more
flexible and sensitive ; ready obediently to
follow the thought, and delicately responsive
to the nature of the subject-matter.   When
one considers how various that subject-matter
is, it will be seen that no literary demand could
well be more exacting.   I am not sure that
the historical scientists would, if they were
pressed, reject some such literary ideal.   But,
in any case, history severed from literature
loses her place and power in the world.   Her
productions become ephemeral ; each fresh fact
that is discovered loosens their precarious hold
on life.

Looking back on the general course of Greek criticism we can see that not a few of its defects may be traced to the fact that the Greeks knew no literature but their own. In the region of literary production they were probably the gainers for being thrown upon their own resources. Their literature must otherwise have lost some of that incomparable freshness which distinguishes it from the other literatures of Europe. It could not have evolved itself on the same natural lines and in such close relation to the organic life of society. But the province of criticism is one of observation and comparison, and a wider comparison would have brought with it an enlarged comprehension. The chief danger, perhaps, which besets a critic is that of attempting to restrict the rights of genius by framing arbitrary canons of literary uniformity. Even Aristotle in the *Poetics* is not free from the failing ; and it may perhaps be questioned whether the highest literary criticism is possible without a knowledge of at least one foreign literature. In the critical appreciation of our own literature no first-rate work was produced till the way had been prepared by the study of Greek and Latin masterpieces. Characteristics long familiar became significant only when light was first flashed on them from the study of antiquity. A lesson even in comparative politics may have a salutary influence on the literary art. In the expiring days of Greece Rome opened up larger horizons to writers who had hitherto been brought up in the seclusion of libraries or in rhetorical schools. The stirrings of political life were now again felt. The *History* of Polybius was one result of this outlook into a wider world. Greek criticism too had showed signs of renewed vitality ; and the return to a sounder taste in the Augustan age is noted by Dionysius of Halicarnassus as due to the invigorating contact of Rome.[1]

It was the confluence of these two civilisations that led to the comparative study of literature in however rudimentary a form. The early experiments were not altogether felicitous.

[1] *De Antiq. Orat.* proem. c. 3.

S

A habit arose of drawing artificial comparisons
between Greek and Roman authors.   Ennius
answered to Homer, Afranius to Menander,
Sallust to Thucydides, Livy to Herodotus.
Still more remote are the analogies suggested
by Plutarch's *Parallel Lives*.   None the less
the method was a true one, and needed only
riper knowledge and judgment to become
fruitful in results.   The first Greek critic who
employed it to any purpose is the author of
the treatise *On the Sublime*.   He has the
unique distinction of drawing his illustrations
from three literatures,—not only from the Greek
and Latin classics, but also, in one passage,
from the Jewish Scriptures (*Gen.* i. 3).[1]

In another respect the same writer approaches to our modern point of view.   He
thinks of literature not merely as a product
of the individual mind, but as an expression of
national life.   Certain conditions are necessary
to produce great thinking and great speaking.

[1] *De Subl.* c. ix. 9 ταύτῃ καὶ ὁ τῶν Ἰουδαίων θεσμοθέτης, οὐχ
ὁ τυχὼν ἀνήρ, . . . εὐθὺς ἐν τῇ εἰσβολῇ γράψας τῶν νόμων
"εἶπεν ὁ Θεός" φησί· τί; "γενέσθω φῶς, καὶ ἐγένετο; γενέσθω
γῆ, καὶ ἐγένετο."

It is not enough that the author should have
the natural gift of beautiful speech, or that he
should have been trained to emulate the great
models of antiquity.   An atmosphere is needed,
a fitting social environment to call forth his
powers.   True as it is that elevation of style
is 'the image reflected from nobility of soul,' [1]
yet noble faculties may be starved for want of
moral sustenance.   What, he asks, are the
causes for the decline of eloquence? for the
'great and world-wide dearth of high utterance
that attends our age'? [2]   Two causes he
assigns, both of them rooted in social conditions.   First, the decay of liberty.   'We
seem to have learnt from infancy that sub-
serviency is the law of life, being from our
tenderest years of thought all but swaddled in
its manners and customs, and having never
tasted that most beautiful and fertile fountain
of eloquence, Freedom—so that we turn out
merely sublime in Courtiership.' [3]   Next, 'the

---

[1] *De Subl.* c. ix. 2 ὕψος μεγαλοφροσύνης ἀπήχημα.

[2] *Ib.* c. xliv. I τοσαύτη λόγων κοσμική τις ἐπέχει τὸν βίον
ἀφορία (Trans. Rhys Roberts).

[3] *Ib.* c. xliv. 3 (Trans. Saintsbury).

love of money and the love of pleasure carry us away into bondage, or rather, as one may say, drown us body and soul in the depths, the love of money causing meanness, and the love of pleasure being the ignoblest of all diseases.' No previous Greek critic, not even Aristotle, had noted the moral atmosphere, the social ideals of an age, as a main factor in the creation of noble works of literature. The only other ancient writer who lays any stress on this topic—now so trite—is Tacitus in the remarkable dialogue *De Oratoribus.*

The inadequate perception of the correspondence between a writer and his age is closely related to what was perhaps the most persistent defect of ancient criticism—a want of historic imagination, of a faculty for apprehending the whole environment of a bygone time. The critic, as we now understand his office, is an interpreter between the present and the past ; he must be imbued with the historic no less than with the literary spirit. Yet it has taken centuries for this idea to be established. It is foreshadowed in Bacon, who in sketching

the principles on which a critical history of
literature should be composed, says that the
writer should 'evoke from the dead as by a
sort of spell the literary genius of the age.'[1]
Not until recent years has either Greek or
English literature been handled in this spirit.
Criticism so practised becomes an art of
constructive imagination.

Nor must we forget that the critic's office
is not completely summed up in the word
'interpretation.' He must needs form a judgment. He cannot renounce this his original
function. If there is such a thing as a standard
of excellence and a tribunal of criticism, the
decisions of that tribunal will admit of intelligent exposition. 'A judgment,' however,
'on literature is'—once more to quote Longinus — 'the final aftergrowth of much endeavour';[2] and the critic is aware that the
ultimate appeal is to Time—to the many not
to the few, to the consentient opinion of

[1] *De Augm. Scient.* B. ii. c. iv. 'ut genius illius temporis
litterarius veluti incantatione quadam a mortuis evocetur.'

[2] *De Subl.* c. vi ἡ γὰρ τῶν λόγων κρίσις πολλῆς ἐστι
πείρας τελευταῖον ἐπιγέννημα (Trans. Saintsbury).

educated mankind. This principle of *Quod
semper quod ubique* in literature is first
enunciated in the treatise *On the Sublime :*

'If then any work on being repeatedly submitted to the judgment of an acute and
cultivated critic, fails to dispose his mind to
lofty ideas ; if it does not leave in the mind
more food for reflection than the words seem
to convey ; and if, the longer you read it, the
less you think of it, there can be here no true
sublimity, when the effect is not sustained
beyond the mere act of perusal. But when a
passage is pregnant in suggestion, when it is
hard, nay, impossible to distract the attention
from it, and when it takes a strong and lasting
hold on the memory, then we may be sure that
we have lighted on the true Sublime. In
general we may regard those words as truly
noble and sublime which please all and please
always. For when the same book produces
the same impression on all who read it, whatever be the difference in their pursuits, their
manner of life, their aspirations, their ages, or
their language, such a harmony of opposites

gives irresistible authority to their favourable verdict.'[1]

This consentient verdict of the ages Greece has gained. In the *Hymn to the Delian Apollo* you may remember the description of the Ionians assembled at their festival : ' Whosoever should meet them at that gathering would deem that they were exempt from death and age for ever, beholding their gracious beauty and rejoicing in heart at the sight of the men and the deep-girdled women.'[2]   What is here said of the Ionians applies with literal truth to the gracious creations of Greek literature—' deathless they are and ageless for ever.'   They are embalmed in writings which possess the greatest of all anti-septic qualities, the quality of style ;—and there lies the answer to the question so often asked : Why can we not be content to read Greek literature in translations ?

Style and thought perfectly blended—it is thus that Pindar's saying comes true : ' The word

[1] *De Subl.* c. vii. 3-4 (Trans. H. L. Havell, Macmillan and Co. 1890).

[2] *Hymn to Delian Apollo*, 151-154.

lives longer than the deeds.'[1]   And it is herein
precisely that the Greeks stand out as the
models of the true literary spirit.   They show
us that he who would worthily pursue the
calling of letters should attempt to rise above
a purely mechanical skill ; that, however lowly
may be the material in which he works, he
must do so in the spirit of the artist, not of
the artisan.   There is of course a weak side to
literary æstheticism.   In *Don Quixote* we read
of a certain author who was renowned for ' the
brilliancy of his prose and the beautiful perplexity
of his expression.'   We seem to know the type.
Let the phrase be but beautiful and rhythmical,
musical and flowing, and it matters not if
the fine words conceal emptiness beneath.   A
literary æsthete was described by Lucian as ' a
strange phantom fed upon dew or ambrosia.'[2]
Him too we know.   His home is not upon the

---

[1] Pind. *Nem.* iv. 6 :

     ῥῆμα δ' ἐργμάτων χρονιώτερον βιοτεύει.

Cp. *Isth.* iii. 58 :

       τοῦτο γὰρ ἀθάνατον φωνᾶεν ἕρπει,

       εἴ τις εὖ εἴπῃ τι.

[2] *Rhet. Prec.* § 11 ξένον φάσμα δρόσῳ ἢ ἀμβροσίᾳ τρεφόμενον.

solid earth.   He sings and soars, he loves and
laments, he knows not what or why ; harmonious
and meaningless is his song.   The cult of
the meaningless is from time to time in the
ascendent.   Once at an exhibition of pictures
I stood in wonder before a certain portrait.   I
begged a friend who was initiated into the
principles of the school to explain it.   The reply
was : ' Think away the head and the face and
you have a residuum of pure colour.'   Whether
this doctrine is to be accepted in painting, and
more particularly in portrait-painting, I do not
know ; but in literature at least it means sure
decay.   Think away the meaning, get rid of
the thought, and you have beautiful and pure
form.   No,—form is essential, but not form without substance.   The supreme merit of the Greeks
is that, on the one hand, they felt and showed
that beauty is of the essence of literature, and
that a formless work of literature is in truth a
misnomer, being dead while yet it lives : it may
have philosophic, it may have scientific merit,
but it will be superseded : what is in it of value
will be incorporated with other works : its sub-

stance is separable from its form.   On the other hand, Greek example reminds us that beauty of form is not all.   The literary writer, whether in prose or verse, is not a maker of fine phrases, a singer in the void.   The Greek poet had something to say, and was not merely concerned how he said it.   He was in close contact with realities.   He drew his sustenance from the soil of human nature.   He touched the springs of national life.   Even the idiom of the people he so used as to ennoble it.   It is the glory of Greek literature that of all literatures it is at once the most artistic and the most popular. And our hope, our best hope, for the literature of the future is, that as the democratic movement extends and calls forth enlarged intellectual sympathies, the old Hellenic harmony may be re-established between that eternal love of beauty on which all art and literature rest, and that love of scientific truth which is the dominant mark of our own age.

Printed by R. & R. CLARK, LIMITED, *Edinburgh*.